Biblical Foundations for Children: Intro to the Pentateuch
By Lenny LaGuardia

Published by Forerunner Publishing
International House of Prayer
3535 E. Red Bridge Road
Kansas City, MO 64137
forerunnerpublishing@ihop.org
IHOP.org

ISBN 13: 978-0-9823262-8-2

Cover design by Isaac Reichenbach

Printed in the United States of America

"Children are like wet cement. What we teach them now will harden and then influence them in decision-making throughout their life. *Biblical Foundations for Children* will give a generation of children tools to grow and thirst after God's Word." —Mike Bickle, Director of the International House of Prayer of Kansas City

"It is a must that we help our children understand that studying the Word of God can be enjoyable." —Lou Engle, Director of TheCall

"*Biblical Foundations for Children* will allow children to be released into having a heart of worship while growing to be all God desires them to be." —Misty Edwards, worship leader at the International House of Prayer of Kansas City

"The hour is upon us to do more than just play games with our children in children's ministry. We need to see them grounded in the deep truths of knowing God so they would grow to preach, teach, and lead their generation unto the Lord." —Allen Hood, Associate Director of the International House of Prayer of Kansas City and president of IHOPU.

"I believe that *Biblical Foundations for Children* is a must for children and Christian educators all across the nations. These lessons will equip children to walk in the knowledge of God." —Daniel Lim, CEO of the International House of Prayer of Kansas City

Dear parents and educators,

I believe that we live in an hour unlike any other, where children must be given the opportunity to be grounded in biblical, foundational truths that come directly from the Word of God. Children growing up today are pulled in many directions to follow false teachings and theologies concerning who God is.

It has been my experience over thirty years of equipping children that we often make a mistake in thinking children can't understand deep truths of the bible. I have often seen educators and even parents soften the truth, thinking the children can't grapple with what appear to be difficult concepts. This has resulted in a generation of children who have grown up knowing about God without truly knowing Him.

This curriculum does not just tell about God; it is meant to lead children into an encounter with God. A unique characteristic of this curriculum that it also leads the communicators through lesson preparation into a rich understanding of and deep experience with God. In this way, they will teach from their heart and experience, which brings spiritual vitality to each lesson. The Word of God does not need to be boring. Many times, children only become bored with God and church when they are not being led into personal encounter with God.

Each lesson in *Biblical Foundations for Children* has four components. First, the teacher preparation component contains all material necessary not only to prepare the lesson, but also to prepare the heart and mind of the teacher. In addition to information about historical and cultural background, archeological insight, and other aspects necessary for a good understanding of each passage studied, a series of questions leads the teacher through the passage devotionally, so that the teacher may encounter the Spirit of God in and through the Bible story. Another section leads the teacher through reflection on that encounter unto sharing the truths of God with the students.

Second, the lesson preparation component contains a template that leads the teacher step by step through preparing to teach the lesson. This template has four sections:. In the *Invitation* section, the teacher reviews information from the previous lesson or lessons that ties into the day's lesson. The new lesson is introduced, and students are invited to meet God through the theme of that lesson. In the *Impartation*, the teacher teaches the story (or stories) from the Word, giving insight and interpretation. In the *Application*, the teacher guides the students through personal application of the truths. Finally, in the *Impact*, there is a summary of the lesson's main truths, focusing on how those truths impact us in our daily life. It includes leading the students in prayer about these truths and their application to our lives. The impact section ends with encouragement to the students concerning how they can walk these truths out during the week and communicate the lesson to their family and friends.

The third component is Car Talk, a take-home paper with several leading questions that parents can use to jump-start discussion of the lesson with the child.

The final component is the at-home pages. These are five daily pages for the student to use to explore further the Bible stories studied on Sunday. These can be used by older students on their own, or parents can use these pages for the basis of family devotions. Homeschooling families can use them as a Bible class curriculum.

May the Lord bless the children that you teach,

Lenny LaGuardia, Executive Director of the Children's Equipping Center and the VP Ministries of the International House of Prayer of Kansas City

Table of Contents

First Quarter, Year One: Biblical Foundations for Children
First Quarter: Intro to the Pentateuch

Objective: To acquaint the student with the origin and historical flow of the Pentateuch so that the student can read any part of the five books and be able to place it in the context of the Hebrew culture and history, while also training the student to recognize and apply biblical truths to his life now.

Goals:
1. Students will learn the value of studying God's words.
2. Students will learn value and use Bible study tools.
3. Students will learn the historical context and customs of the Pentateuch.
4. Students will learn the timeline of the Pentateuch.
5. Students will be able to tell some of the stories of the Pentateuch.
6. Students will be able to find truths in the stories of the Pentateuch to apply to their own lives.
7. Students will be able to recite the names of the books of the Pentateuch, as well as the basic content of each book.

Lesson preparation methodology:

This teacher's manual is designed both to equip you to prepare your lesson presentation and to lead you into encounter with the Lord so that you can lead your students to encounter Him.

You will read an objective statement that summarizes the lesson's intent.

Then you will find a biblical foundations section. This is information and study material for you to master in a devotional setting. Our hope is that you will encounter God in the study of these truths. As you study, continue to ask the Lord what truths your students need to hear at this time.

The third segment is the presentation preparation, where you take what you have learned and what you have heard from the Lord, and prepare your presentation, using the outline template provided.

In the follow-up segment, you continue to bring your students before the Lord in prayer, particularly concerning the truths you are going to teach them.

Materials needed:

1. Each student should have a Bible, a notebook, and a pencil.
2. Timeline provided in the packet.
3. A wall map of the Middle East during Old Testament times.

First Quarter, Year One: Through the Bible in Four Years
Lesson One:
Intro to the Pentateuch: Genesis

Objective: To introduce the student to the Pentateuch and the book of Genesis.

Key verse for this lesson: "Then God said, 'Let us make man in our own image, in our likeness, and let them rule over the fish of the sea and the birds of the air, over the livestock, over all the earth, and over all the creatures that move along the ground.' So God created man in his own image; in the image of God He created him; male and female created He them." (Gen. 1:26-27)

Key thoughts to consider and to pass on:
    A. God created man in His own image because He desired them to be His family.
    B. God's purpose for man on earth is to rule over the rest of creation.

Biblical Foundation

I. Background information on the Pentateuch

"The 'Pentateuch' is a term used to describe the first five books of the Old Testament (Genesis-Deuteronomy). In the Jewish Scriptures these books are referred to as the Law, or Torah, a Hebrew word that means 'guide' or 'instruction.' But the Pentateuch includes more than just laws. The great narratives of the Pentateuch tell the story of creation, of God's choosing of a special people (Israel), and of the person God chose to lead these people out of slavery in Egypt. This leader, Moses, received from God the laws and instructions that were to guide Israel's life and worship. Along with these stories, several other important events are recorded in the Pentateuch, including the choosing of Abraham and Sarah to be Israel's earliest ancestors, the escape from slavery in Egypt, and the wandering of the people of Israel through the desert to the edge of the land God promised to give them.

The Pentateuch begins at the 'beginning,' with stories about how God created the world and its people (Gen. 1-5). This is followed by the story of Noah and the great flood and a story explaining why there are different human languages (Gen 6-11). In Genesis 12 the history of God's people (later known as Israel) begins with God's choosing of Abraham and his wife Sarah to leave their home and go to a new land (Canaan). God promised Abraham that his descendants would become a great nation and would eventually make the land of Canaan their home (Gen. 12:1-3; 17:1-8). The remainder of Genesis describes how the promises God made to Abraham and Sarah began to be worked out in their descendants, including Isaac, Jacob, and their families.

As Exodus begins, however, these promises are in question because Abraham and Sarah's descendants are living as slaves in Egypt. But God hears the people begging for help and chooses Moses to lead the people out of Egypt (Ex. 3:4-12). This great event, known as the 'exodus,' is told in exciting detail in the book of Exodus. Israel's time of slavery in Egypt became a reminder to future generations: because God cared about the people of Israel and responded to them when they were suffering and oppressed, they were to treat others, especially the poor and powerless, with fairness and justice (Exodus 23:6-9; Leviticus 25:35-38; Deuteronomy 5:6,12-15).

The second major event in Exodus is the agreement (covenant) that the LORD made with Moses and the people of Israel at Mount Sinai. In this agreement, God gives the laws and instructions that would guide how the people were to live and worship. God had chosen them and then brought them out of Egypt. At Sinai, God made it clear what the people of Israel must do in order to show that they were God's "holy" people. These laws and instructions are found in Exodus 20-40; Leviticus; selected portions of Numbers; and in Moses' sermons in Deuteronomy. The remainder of Numbers tells about the years the people spent wandering through the desert on their way to the promised land of Canaan. The narratives in this book focus on the way the LORD God continued to care for the people even in the terrible years they spent in the desert. The Pentateuch ends with the people of Israel camped in Moab just across the Jordan River from Canaan, ready to enter the land God had promised to their ancestors."[1]

Pentateuch means "five-volumed book." Because the main human figure of the Pentateuch is Moses, these books have traditionally been called the "Books of Moses." The question of what person or persons wrote these books is still discussed by historians and biblical scholars. But based on the manuscripts that currently exist, it is not likely that the question of authorship can be answered with any degree of certainty. Jewish tradition and the Bible itself affirm Moses as the overall author. Information concerning the death of Moses was, in all likelihood, written by Joshua. Listing of kings who were not alive during the lifetime of Moses and other notes such as indicating that a particular city is still named that "even to this day" suggest that as scribes copied the books of Moses, they added a few updating notes here and there. However, evangelical Christianity holds to Moses as the author of the Pentateuch.

II. Content of the Pentateuch[2]

A. Overall: from the creation of the cosmos through the preliminary conquest of the
           promised land (Canaan)
B. General content of the individual books
    1. Genesis—the beginning of history and the beginning of the nation of Israel
    2. Exodus—call of Moses, exodus from Egypt, and beginning of law
    3. Leviticus—primarily laws for society and worship
    4. Numbers—wilderness wanderings and preliminary conquest of land plus additional laws
    concerning society and worship
    5. Deuteronomy—last will and testament of Moses—summarizes history and law and
        presents a new interpretation of the law for a new generation which will have to apply it to
        a different life and place
   C. Interpretation of the Pentateuch

---

[1] American Bible Society, "Introduction to the Pentateuch," www.americanbible.org/absport/news/item.php?id=61
[2] Based on Bob Dunston's "Introduction to the Torah," http://religion.ucumberlands.edu/hebrew_bible/hbnotes/tornotes.htm

1. Usually revolves around the promises to Abraham in Genesis 12:1-3 and how those promises moved toward fulfillment

2. Elements to remember in interpretation

    a. Story

        i. A substantial portion of the Pentateuch is story—stories invite the reader into a world and time different from the world and time of the reader

        ii. Not every element and detail of a story is significant—the story as a whole has meaning; thus, the story must be read as a whole and not interpreted as a series of details

        iii. Stories flesh out theology and make it applicable in real life

    b. Law verse legalism

        i. Law does not necessarily mean legalism, though there are many regulations and rules in the Torah, legalism or a legalistic faith was not the intended response

        ii. The law can only be fulfilled through grace

        iii. God gave the law to Israel because He loved Israel and wanted to enjoy a relationship with Israel

        iv. The law provided a way for Israel and for God to be related to each other

        v. The law was not meant to terrorize or enslave Israel, but to lead them to the need for a savior

    c. The Pentateuch is foundational

        i. The Pentateuch sets the stage for the rest of the Hebrew Bible, as well as the New Testament—it defines Israel, God's relationship with Israel, and Israel's relationship with God—it is to the Hebrew Bible what the Gospels are to the New Testament

        ii. Jesus and the rabbis quoted extensively from the Pentateuch.

        iii. Paul tells us in I Corinthians 10:6 that all that happened to Israel served as an example for the believers

III. The Book of Genesis

    A. The name

    The word "Genesis" is from the Greek, *geneseos*, found in the Septuagint (the Greek translation of the Old Testament). It can mean "birth" or "history of origin," depending on the context. In the original Hebrew, each book is known by the first phrase of the book. Hence, the Hebrew name is *bereshith*, or "in the beginning." Since it is a book describing the beginnings of the world, the human race, and the nation of Israel, it is aptly named in both Hebrew and Greek.

    B. Author and date of writing

    Jews and Christians have believed for centuries that Moses wrote Genesis. There was also apparently some editorial updating done by scribes over the centuries from the time of Moses until the Pentateuch reached its present form as compiled by Jewish scholars in the Masoretic texts (AD 800-1200).

    Genesis, as well as the rest of the Pentateuch, was written by Moses during the forty years of wandering in the wilderness. How would Moses know with such accuracy details of events which happened long before his time? First, we know from his own account that he often met with God in the tabernacle and spoke with God "as a friend to a friend." Surely God could have related the details to Moses just as He did the law on Mount Sinai. Second, the ancient people had a strong oral tradition. Even today, in tribal situations where history and genealogies are communicated orally, people can recount their own genealogy back to as many as 100 generations. Studies have shown that an oral tradition is passed from generation to generation with great accuracy and detail. So Moses, having been trained in reading and writing by the Egyptians, could well have been recording the historical stories of his people, then continuing to record events as an ongoing history.

C. Archaeological confirmation
The customs and style of chapters 1-38 closely relate to what archeologists have found in ancient Mesopotamian life, culture, and writings. Chapters 39-50 indicate Egyptian experience and influence.

D. Theological theme and message
Genesis is a book of beginnings. The beginning of the world, of light and darkness, the planets and stars, the earth and all on the earth. We also read of the beginning of the human family, the institution of marriage, the entrance of sin, and the beginnings of society and civilization. We see the beginning of many relationships: between God and man, man and man, and man and creation.

In Genesis we first see the need for a redeemer in the fall of man, are given the first promise of a coming redeemer as the one glimmer of hope given in the curse, and see the first provision of a substitute in the sacrificial ram substitute for Isaac.

It is clear that Moses wrote this as an historical account, for ten times he uses this word. "This is the account of the heavens and the earth when they were created . . . " "This is the account of Adam's line . . . " Ten times we find this literary structure: Genesis 2:4; 5:1; 6:9; 10:1; 11:10; 11:27; 25:12; 25:19; 36:1; and 37:2. The first five accounts take us from the creation of the world to Terah, Abraham's father. This is the account of God creating people and these people spreading out over the face of the earth. The second five take us from Abraham through the lives of his sons, grandsons, and great-grandsons. This is the account of God selecting a particular people to be his own and through whom blessing will come to all the people of His creation.

A Detailed Outline of Genesis[3]

I. The beginning of history
    A. The creation story (1:1-2:25)
        1. Mankind as end of creation (1:1-2:4a)

---

[3] Bob Dunston, "Outline of Genesis," http://religion.ucumberlands.edu/hebrew_bible/hbout/genout.htm

    2. Mankind as center of creation (2:4b-25)
  B. Fall of Adam and Eve (3:1-24)
  C. Cain and Abel (4:1-26)
  D. Descendants of Adam (5:1-32)
  E. Flood narrative (6:1-9:29)
  F. Genesis of nations (10:1-32)
  G. Tower of Babel (11:1-9)
  H. Genealogy of Abraham (11:10-32)

II. The beginning of the nation of Israel
  A. Abraham (12:1-25:18)
    1. Promises to Abram (12:1-9)
    2. Abram in Egypt (12:10-20)
    3. Abram and Lot separate (13:1-18)
    4. Abram rescues Lot (14:1-16)
    5. Abram and Melchizedek (14:17-24)
    6. Promises renewed (15:1-21)
    7. Birth of Ishmael (16:1-16)
    8. Covenant of circumcision (17:1-27)
    9. Fate of Sodom and Gomorrah (18:1-19:38)
    10. Abram and Abimelech (20:1-18)
    11. Birth of Isaac (21:1-7)
    12. Dismissal of Hagar and Ishmael (21:8-21)
    13. Covenant with Abimelech (21:22-34)
    14. Near sacrifice of Isaac (22:1-24)
    15. Death of Sarah (23:1-20)
    16. Securing a wife for Isaac (24:1-67)
    17. Abraham's other sons (25:1-6)
    18. Death of Abraham (25:7-11)
    19. Descendants of Ishmael (25:12-18)
  B. Isaac (25:19-26:35)
    1. Birth of Esau and Jacob (25:19-26)
    2. Favoritism (25:27-28)
    3. Esau sells his birthright (25:29-34)
    4. Isaac and Abimelech (26:1-16)
    5. Trouble with wells (26:17-22)
    6. Covenant with God (26:23-25)
    7. Covenant with Abimelech (26:26-33)
    8. Esau finds wives (26:34-35)
  C. Jacob (27:1-36:43)
    1. Tension between Jacob and Esau
      a. Jacob steals the blessing (27:1-40)
      b. Jacob is sent away (27:41-28:5)
      c. Esau marries an Ishmaelite woman (28:6-9)

2. Dream at Bethel (28:10-22)
3. Tension between Jacob and Laban (29:1-30)
     a. Jacob finds a wife (29:1-20)
     b. Jacob tricked by Laban (29:21-29)
     c. Favoritism (29:30)
4. The birth of Jacob's children (29:31-30:24)
5. Uneasy reconciliation between Jacob and Laban (31:1-32:21)
     a. Jacob's flocks increase (20:25-43)
     b. Jacob leaves Laban (31:1-29)
     c. Uneasy reconciliation (31:30-55)
     d. Preparation to meet Esau (32:1-21)
6. Wrestling with God at Peniel (32:22-32)
7. Uneasy reconciliation with Esau (33:1-20)
8. Later, difficult years (34:1-36:43)
     a. Rape of Dinah (34:1-31)
     b. Covenant renewed (35:1-15)
     c. Birth of Benjamin, death of Rachel (35:16-21)
     d. Sons of Jacob (35:22-26)
     e. Death of Isaac (35:27-29)
     f. Descendants of Esau (36:1-43)

D. Joseph (37:1-50:26)
1. Early life (37:1-36)
     a. Favoritism (37:1-4)
     b. Joseph's dreams (37:5-11)
     c. Capture and selling of Joseph (37:12-36)
2. Judah and Tamar (38:1-30)
3. Joseph's rise to power in Egypt (39:1-41:57)
     a. Joseph's experiences in Potiphar's household (39:1-18)
     b. Joseph confined to prison (39:19-23)
     c. Joseph interprets dreams (40:1-23)
     d. Joseph interprets Pharaoh's dreams (41:1-36)
     e. Joseph elevated to power (41:37-57)
4. Joseph in power in Egypt (42:1-50:26)
     a. Joseph's brothers' first trip to Egypt (42:1-38)
     b. Joseph's brothers' second trip to Egypt (43:1-34)
     c. Testing of the brothers (44:1-34)
     d. Joseph revealed (45:1-15)
     e. Jacob invited to come to Egypt (45:16-28)
     f. Jacob comes to Egypt (46:1-7)
     g. Names of those who came (46:8-27)
     h. Reunion of Jacob and Joseph (46:28-34)
     i. Jacob and Pharaoh (47:1-12)
     j. Joseph's famine policies (47:13-26)
5. Deaths of Jacob and Joseph (47:27-50:26)

      a. Jacob prepares to die (47:27-31)
      b. Jacob blesses Joseph's sons (48:1-22)
      c. Jacob blesses his sons (49:1-27)
      d. Death of Jacob (49:28-33)
      e. Burial of Jacob (50:1-14)
      f. Uneasy reconciliation between Joseph and his brothers (50:15-21)
      g. Joseph's last words and death (50:22-26)

Simplified Outline:

I. The beginning of history
      A. Creation (1:1-2:25)
      B. Fall of Adam and Eve (3:1-24)
      C. Cain and Abel (4:1-26)
      D. Descendants of Adam (5:1-32)
      E. The flood (6:1-9:29)
      F. Genesis of nations (10:1-32)
      G. Tower of Babel (11:1-9)
      H. Genealogy of Abraham (11:10-32)

II. The beginning of the nation of Israel
      A. Abraham (12:1-25:18)
      B. Isaac (25:19-26:35)
      C. Jacob (27:1-36:43)
      D. Joseph (37:1-50:26)

Lesson Presentation Preparation

You will use the following Lesson Presentation outline template. In this next step, prayerfully fill this in to prepare your teaching lesson.

Part One of your lesson will be to introduce this theme and lesson, then invite your students into God's heart for them in and through this topic. For example, after telling them that for the next three months the class will be studying the first five books of the Bible, you might invite them to know God's great desire to communicate to each one of them. You might explain that the same God who spoke the truth in these books to Moses is the same God who wants to speak to each of them. Remind them of the purpose of God's Word—to reveal Himself to them and draw them into relationship with Him.

Communicate your love of the Word to your students. Don't be afraid to show your enthusiasm for studying the Bible. Remember, more is caught than taught. Your enthusiasm for God and His Word will inspire your students to make the study of the Word a priority in their own life. As you consider how best to invite your students into the study of the Word, pray for God to show you the way into their hearts. Is there any story from your own life that will draw them in?

Part Two of your lesson will be to invite those you teach into the knowledge of God through His Word. Because this lesson is an introduction and overview lesson, it may be a bit different from the usual session where you teach from the Word. Remember that the introduction and overview lessons form the backbone or timeline on which the students will place the stories and teachings of the Bible, so it is important to present the information in a way that the students will easily grasp and retain it.

Again, show your enthusiasm. For lessons like this one, it's important to make it fun, too. Be animated when you explain the outline overview of Genesis. Get participation from your students, too. Make them a part of the teaching.

Part Three of your lesson is the application. Here you will help those you teach identify areas of their lives where they can apply God's Word and His emotions. They may identify attitudes to change, behaviors to stop or start, new ways of thinking about things. Your job is to guide them into this discovery and to encourage them to take the step of application and change.

Part Four of your lesson is to assist and guide those you teach as they commit to action plans that will enable them to apply and communicate what they have learned in the lesson to impact and influence their family, friends, schools, neighborhoods, and the nations for God.

THEME: *The Pentateuch*

Lesson 1: *Introduction to the Pentateuch and Genesis*

Part One: The Invitation

A. Introduce the unit theme and the lesson for today. Depending on the age of your students, you might simply read the key verse, *or* you might ask your students to memorize one or both of the verses.

B. Ask your students what they think when they hear the words, "Bible Study." Have several students share their thoughts.

C. Share with your students a bit about your own journey concerning studying the Word. Write yourself a few notes here about your own experiences and what studying the Bible means to you.

1. My experiences concerning studying the Word include . . .

2. To me, studying the Bible means . . . .

3. To me, studying the Bible excites me because . . . .

4. Studying the Word has changed me in the following ways . . .

D. Invite your students to join you on the journey of hearing from God through His Word.

Part Two: The Impartation

I. Introduction

A. Have the students open their Bibles to the table of contents. Point out the Old Testament books and the New Testament books. Have the students read the names of the first five books of the Old Testament together. Chant these five names together several times.

Note: You might play a game where you point randomly to students. The first student pointed to says, "Genesis." The second says, "Exodus," and so on.

B. Introduce the word, "Pentateuch." Encourage your students to take some notes in their notebook as you teach. Help them know what to write by indicating to them words or phrases they might write down, and spell any difficult words for them. You might also want to make a large flash card for words such as "Pentateuch" and "Genesis."

Using the resource notes, write here what you will tell them.

    1. The meaning of the name and to what it refers

    2. The books in the Pentateuch

    3. An overall outline or flow of the Pentateuch. You might have the timeline posted on the wall and point to times on the line to explain when each book of the Pentateuch takes place. Pointing out the places on a map of the Middle East during Old Testament times would be helpful in assisting the students to identify where each book takes place.

List here the general information you will mention for each book:

    1. Genesis:

    2. Exodus:

    3. Leviticus:

    4. Numbers:

    5. Deuteronomy:

C. Explain the significance of studying the Pentateuch and why it helps us to understand the rest of the Bible.

D. Introduce the first book of the Pentateuch: Genesis.

Ask your students to turn to Genesis 1. Read aloud the first verse.

      1. Explain the name of the book both in English and in Hebrew.

      2. Explain how it is a book of beginnings. List for them some of the beginnings that we see in the book.

      3. Talk about the author of the book and when he wrote it.

      4. Ask your students how they think Moses could have known about events that happened long before he was born, like creation. Let several students respond. Then explain the two ways he might have known.

5. Share the simple outline of the book. As you go over each point, attach the appropriate picture to the time line.

> The beginning of history
> > i. Creation
> > ii. Fall of Adam and Eve
> > iii. Cain and Abel
> > iv. Descendants of Adam
> > v. The flood
> > vi. Genesis of nations
> > vii. Tower of Babel
> > viii. Genealogy of Abraham

E. After this, go back over the basic events of Genesis, and teach the motions for the following events (hand and arm motions are given in the appendix):

> Creation
> Fall
> Flood
> Tower of Babel
> Nations scatter
> Abraham
> Isaac
> Jacob
> Joseph
> To Egypt

Have students stand and practice the motions while saying the events (in order).

Part Three: The Application

Ask the students to write answers to the following questions in their journals.

1. How do you think God can speak to you through the book of Genesis?

2. Do you think it is important to read the Bible every day? Why?

3. Is there any time of the day when you take time to read the Bible?

4. What things keep you from reading the Bible?

5. When do you think would be a good time for you to read the Bible every day?

Part Four: The Impact

A. Explain to your students that God wants to speak to them every day through His Word. Ask those who want to receive His grace and help to study His Word to stand up. Lead them in the following prayer:

Father, I know that You want to speak to me. I am so glad that You do! I value Your Words. Holy Spirit, help me to study the Word of God. I ask you to give me grace to read Your Word every day. I ask You for wisdom and revelation to understand Your Word and to apply it to my life. Reveal Yourself to me through Your Word. I want to see You in the Bible. Jesus, you are the Living Word of God. Let me see you in the written Word.

Father, I ask for grace to live according to the truths of your Word. Help me to share the stories and truths of Your Word with my family and friends. I thank You for Your Word and Your desire to have fellowship with me. In Jesus' name, Amen.

B. Close by encouraging your students to share with their family what they have learned today.
1. Suggest that they have their parents help them practice saying the five books of the Pentateuch and reciting the main events of Genesis with the hand motions. If you have time, have them recite the five books with you and the main events of Genesis.
2. Hand out the Car Talk papers. Explain that every week they will get a Car Talk paper to give to their parents for use in the car on the way home from church.
3. Introduce your students to Forerunner Kids Club. Explain that the daily At-Home sheets are located there for them to download and do every day.

CAR TALK

Questions to jump-start conversation with your 7- to 12-year-old on the way home from church:

1. I hear you learned about the Pentateuch in class today. That's a big word! What does *Pentateuch* mean?

2. So it means "five books"? Can you name them? (They learned them in class today, but may need a little help remembering all five.)

3. How about the events of Genesis? Can you remember those? I hear that you have hand motions that go with them.

This week's memory verse: "Then God said, 'Let us make man in our own image, in our likeness, and let them rule over the fish of the sea and the birds of the air, over the livestock, over all the earth, and over all the creatures that move along the ground.' So God created man in his own image; in the image of God He created him; male and female created He them." (Gen. 1:26-27)

Practice saying the first five books of the Bible and the main events/people of Genesis using hand motions.

THEME: *The Pentateuch*

Lesson 1: *Introduction to the Pentateuch and Genesis*

Day One: Genesis 1

I. Read Genesis chapter 1. As you do, answer the following:

    A. What was the world like in the beginning?

    B. Where was the Spirit of God?

    C. What happened on the first day?

    D. What happened on the second day?

    E. What happened on the third day?

    F. What happened on the fourth day?

    G. What happened on the fifth day?

    H. What happened on the sixth day?

    I. What happened on the seventh day?

    J. What pattern did God use when He created man and woman?

    K. What did God think about His creation?

II.   Think about these things and write down your thoughts.

    A. Why do you think God decided to create mankind and a world for us to live in?

    B. Is there anything that makes men and women special compared to the rest of creation? If so, what?

    C. What does the account of creation tell you about God?

THEME: *The Pentateuch*

Lesson 1: *Introduction to the Pentateuch and Genesis*

Day Two: Genesis 2

I. Read Genesis chapter 2. As you do, answer the following:

A. What happened on the seventh day?

B. Of what did God form the first man?

C. Where did God put him?

D. What was his job?

E. What instruction did God give the man?

F. What did God notice about the man when he was by himself in the garden?

G. Why did God bring the animals to the man?

H. Did the man find a suitable helper among the animals?

I. What did God do next?

J. What did the man think about the woman whom God had made?

II.   Think about these things and write down your thoughts.

A. When God blessed the seventh day and made it holy, it means that He set it apart as a special day. What do you think is special about this seventh day that we observe on Sundays?

B. Why do you think God gave the man just one rule—the rule about not eating from the one tree?

C. Why do you think God thought it was not good for man to be alone? What does this tell you about the emotions and feelings of God? Do you think God ever felt lonely?

THEME: *The Pentateuch*

Lesson 1: *Introduction to the Pentateuch and Genesis*
Day Three: Genesis 3:1-13

I. Read Genesis chapter 3:1-13. As you do, answer the following:

    A. How does Moses describe the serpent?

    B. What did the serpent ask the woman?

    C. What did the woman answer?

    D. Did God really tell the man that he could not even touch the tree? Look at Gen. 2:17.

    E. Did the serpent think they would die? What did he say would happen?

    F. When the woman looked at the fruit, what did she think about it?

    G. When she reached out her hand and touched it, did she die?

    H. Do you think this led her to doubt that God would punish her for eating the fruit?

    I. What happened when she and her husband ate the fruit?

    J. What did they do when God came?

    K. What did God say when they were hiding?

    L. What else did God ask them?

II.   Think about these things and write down your thoughts.

    A. God told the man not to eat from the tree, and the man told his wife not to eat, not even to touch it. Did adding to what God commanded help keep the woman from sin or did it make it easier for her to sin? Should we try to help people obey God's commands by adding more commands to them?

    B. Did God really not know where the man was when he was hiding? Why do you think God asked him where he was, instead of ordering him to come out?

    C. The man was hiding, but when God asked, "Where are you?" he said, "Here I am!" Why do you think he answered God instead of staying quiet and hidden? When you sin, do you hide from God or run to Him? How do you think God feels about you when you sin?

THEME: *The Pentateuch*

Lesson 1: *Introduction to the Pentateuch and Genesis*
Day Four: Genesis 3:14-24

I. Read Genesis chapter 3:14-24. As you do, answer the following:

    A. What was the curse upon the serpent?
        1. How will he walk now?

        2. "enmity between" means that they became enemies. Who became enemies?

        3. What would the serpent do to a descendant of the woman?

        4. What would that man, that descendant of the woman, do to the serpent?

    B. What was the curse upon the woman?
        1. What would be increased?

        2. The Hebrew word used for "desire" means "desire to rule over."
          i. What would the wife desire?

          ii. Whom did God appoint as the head of the household?

    C. What was the curse upon the man?
        1. God cursed something else when He punished the man. What was it?

        2. What happened to the earth because of that curse?

        3. How did the curse affect the man?

        4. Did the man have to work before the curse?

        5. So how did the curse affect his job?

    D. What did the man name himself and his wife?

    E. God made them clothes. From what did He make the clothes?

    F. Why did God put Adam and Eve out of the Garden of Eden?

II.   Think about these things and write down your thoughts.

    A. Since man had now fallen into sin, what do you think the world would be like if sinful man could live forever?

    B. Who do you think was the descendant of the woman who crushed the head of the serpent?

THEME: *The Pentateuch*

Lesson 1: *Introduction to the Pentateuch and Genesis*
Day Five: Genesis 4:1-16

I. Read Genesis chapter 4:1-16. As you do, answer the following:

    A. What was name of Adam's first son? What was his job?

    B. What was the name of Adam's second son? What was his job?

    C. What did Abel bring as an offering to the Lord? What did Cain bring?

    D. How did God feel about their offerings?

    E. Did Cain receive the correction of the Lord?

    F. What did Cain decide to do about it?

    G. How did Cain react when God asked him about Abel?

    H. What did Adam's blood do?

    I. How did God punish Cain for what he did?

    J. How did Cain relate to the presence of God after this?

II.   Think about these things and write down your thoughts.

    A. If Cain had responded by bringing the correct kind of offering, do you think God would have received him and blessed him?

    B. Twice in this story we see God bring correction to Cain. Does Cain respond with repentance and humility? How do you respond to correction or discipline?

    C. Cain had a problem; he brought the wrong type of offering. But he blamed Abel for it and so he killed Abel. When you do something wrong, do you admit your problem and take the consequences? Or, do you find it easy to blame other people?

    D. Why don't you pray right now and ask God for grace to receive correction with humility, to admit your fault, to receive consequences humbly, and to repent when God convicts you of sin.

First Quarter, Year One: Biblical Foundations for Children
Lesson Two:
Genesis: God's Desire for a Family

Objective: To introduce the student to a main biblical theme which begins in the book of Genesis—that God is a Father who desires a family.

Key verse for this lesson: "If you do what is right, will you not be accepted? But if you do not do what is right, sin is crouching at your door; it desires to have you, but you must master it." (Gen. 4:7)

Key thoughts to consider and to pass on:

1. God created man in His own image because He desired them to be His family.
2. God created man and woman with an innocent spirit and free will. He gave them opportunity to choose between good and evil, between obedience and disobedience.
3. Even though God knew man would choose sin, God already had a plan to restore us to fellowship with Him.

Review from last week:

I. The beginning of history
     A. Creation (1:1-2:25)
     B. Fall of Adam and Eve (3:1-24)
     C. Cain and Abel (4:1-26)
     D. Descendants of Adam (5:1-32)
     E. The flood (6:1-9:29)
     F. Genesis of nations (10:1-32)
     G. Tower of Babel (11:1-9)
     H. Genealogy of Abraham (11:10-32)

II. The beginning of the nation of Israel
     A. Abraham (12:1-25:18)
     B. Isaac (25:19-26:35)
     C. Jacob (27:1-36:43)
     D. Joseph (37:1-50:26)

Biblical Foundation

I. Read Genesis chapters 1-9. As you do, journal your answers to the following questions. Because this is an extended passage, you could work on two Bible chapters a day so that you have ample time to pray and reflect over the Word.

    A. What is God's heart and emotion towards His creation in chapter 1?

    B. When God sees Adam alone in the garden, what is God's thought and feeling towards Adam? What does God desire for Adam to experience rather than loneliness?

    C. What is God's purpose in creating Eve? Or in other words, what is Eve's chief purpose?

    D. In the evening, God would manifest Himself in the Garden and walk with Adam and Eve. Why do you think He would do this?

    E. If you had been Adam or Eve, how do you think you would have felt to have the Creator God walking with you at your side, conversing?

    F. What do you think they might have talked about?

    G. If you had the opportunity to walk with God as they did, what would you want to talk about?

    H. How do you think God felt after Adam and Eve ate the forbidden fruit?

    I. How do you think God felt when He had to curse them as a consequence of their sin?

    J. How do you think God felt when He had to throw them out of the garden and could no longer take walks with them in the evenings? How do you think Adam and Eve felt?

K. In chapter 4, we find that God gave Adam, Eve, and their children a way to fellowship with Him through sacrifices. How do you think God felt when He saw Abel offer the sacrifice which He had commanded?

L. How do you think He felt when Cain offered the first fruits of his own labor, even though it was not the commanded sacrifice?

    1. Why do you think Cain chose to do this?

    2. Was God confronting Cain's action and attitude to judge him or to woo him?

M. Do you think God had feelings of justice when He confronted Cain over Abel's blood, or do you think God felt the pain of a father over two sons in conflict? What does this suggest about the emotions and desire of God?

N. Genesis 5 lists more genealogies. Why do you think God was concerned about recording the progression of families, of fathers and sons? What does this suggest about God's feelings concerning family?

O. Read Genesis 6:5-8 a second time.

    1. Write down all the "emotion" words that describe how God felt.

    2. Why do you think it grieved God that He had made man? Do you think He was more grieved that He had created or that His creation had given themselves over to sin and were mistreating each other? How does the fact that He chose to save a family to start over help us see the direction of His grief?

3. Noah found favor in the eyes of the Lord. Imagine God looking over all the sin, all the people engaged in sin, and one man stands out—Noah. Notice that in verse 9, not only are we told that Noah is a righteous man, but we are also told he is a father; he has three sons. What does this mean to you?

P. Out of all the people and families on the earth at that time, God chooses to save one family and begin again through them. One father, three sons, and the wives. Think about this. Here He chooses to use one family to bring the human race back to Him, to start over as it were. What are your thoughts about this?

II. Look back over Genesis 3-9. For each story, write down the basic facts or events of the story:

A. Creation and the creation of man

B. The fall of man

C. Cain and Abel

D. Noah and the flood

III. Reflect upon the following:

    A. Through this study, what has God spoken to you about:

        1. His emotions

        2. His feelings and desires concerning a family of His own

        3. His eternal purposes

    B. Finish these sentences:

        1. What really struck me when I read about creation was...

        2. When I studied the fall of man, what stood out to me was...

        3. What struck me in the story of Cain and Abel was...

4. Although I've heard the story of Noah and the flood before,
 what I realized this time was...

5. Through the study of Genesis 1-9, God spoke to me about...

IV. Map Time

While we do not know the exact location of the garden of Eden, we know the rivers near it. Based on the reference to the Euphrates and Tigris (Hidekel) River, most Bible teachers place the garden of Eden in the Middle East.

So when you teach, locate for your students:
1. The garden of Eden—near where the Euphrates and Tigris join together. On the map below, look near the "S" of SUMER.
2. For Noah, we don't really know where he lived, either. You can point out where the ark landed, in the mountains of Ararat.

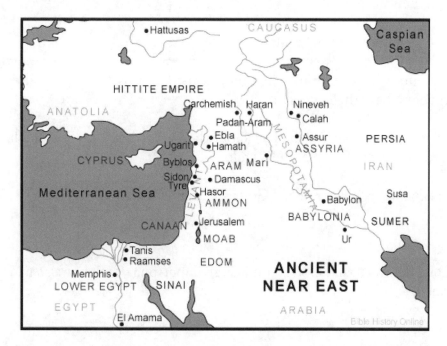

THEME: *The Pentateuch*
Lesson 2: *Genesis: God's desire for a family*

Part One: The Invitation

A. Review the unit theme.

    1. Unit theme:

    2. Lead your students in reciting the names of the five books of the Pentateuch.

    3. Lead your students in reciting the main events of Genesis, with hand motions:

Creation	Abraham
Fall	Isaac
Flood	Jacob
Tower of Babel	Joseph
Nations scatter	To Egypt

    4. Introduce today's lesson topic and explain how it is one of the central themes of the Bible.

        a. Lesson topic:

        b. Memory verse for today:

C. Ask the students what they think when they hear the words, "God is a Family Man." Have several students share their thoughts.

D. Share with your students what you feel about the Father-heart of God and how you have experienced His desire for you as His child.

    1. One time when I experienced God as Father was...

    2. To me, the truth that God is not just an impersonal God, but also a loving Father is exciting because...

E. Invite your students to meet with God and His desire for a family as He shows this to us in the early chapters of Genesis.

Part Two: The Impartation

I. Things to consider as you prepare:
    A. There are several ways in which you might approach presenting this lesson.
        1. You might pick one story and focus on it, bringing out the theme while teaching the details of the story.
        2. You might give an overview of the four stories, focusing on the theme as it appears in each story.

    B. There are various methods of presentation.
        1. You might use drama.
            a. If your class is large enough, you could split into three or four groups, with an adult leading each group.
                i. Give each group a different story to act out: creation; the fall; Cain and Abel; Noah and the flood.
                ii. Use ten to fifteen minutes for each group to learn their story.
                iii. Call the groups together. Have each group present their story to the rest.
                iv. At the end, summarize and draw conclusions and applications, particularly concerning God's desire for a family.
            b. If you have a small group, you might focus on one or two stories.

        2. You might use storytelling, where you tell the story in a dramatic tone of voice, using gestures. You might focus on one story, then bring out teaching points, or you might use several of the stories. As you tell the stories, go one by one and after each story bring out a main teaching point or two related to the theme of God's desire for a family.

        3. You might use a mix of the two, where you tell the story, but you have students act it out in front of the others as you tell the story and direct them into their places.

II. Preparing the impartation segment:

        1. The method I will use:

        2. The story/stories I will use:

III. The Impartation:

Introduce the stories you will be teaching today: creation, the fall of man, Cain and Abel, and Noah. Put those pictures up on the timeline at the very start of the timeline, one after another. For Noah, put the picture about three or four inches to the right of Cain and Abel.

Show the students where on the map these events probably took place: in the area near where the Euphrates and the Tigris come together.

A. First story

    1. Telling the story:

    2. Truths to which I will draw my students' attention:

B. Second story

    1. Telling the story:

    2. Truths to which I will draw my students' attention:

C. Third story

    1.   Telling the story:

    2. Truths to which I will draw my students' attention:

D. Fourth story

    1.   Telling the story:

    2. Truths to which I will draw my students' attention:

Part Three: The Application

Ask the students to write answers to the following questions in their journals.

  1. Why do you think God created the world and human beings?

  2. If you were God, and your creation disobeyed your command and chose to break their fellowship with you, how would you feel? What might you do?

  3. Since God created people to become a part of His family, if you have received Jesus as your Savior, then you are a part of God's family. How do you think God feels about you?

Depending on which story/stories you used in your lesson, select a few questions from the questions you answered in the Biblical Foundation section.

Part Four: The Impact

  A. Explain to your students that, since God wants us to be a part of His family, but our sin separates us from God, He came up with a plan to reunite us with Him. He sent Jesus to take upon Himself the punishment that we deserve. That punishment is eternal separation from God. When Jesus died on the cross, He not only died physically, but He was also separated from God the Father—something that had never happened to Him before. When this happened, Jesus cried out, "My God, My God, why have You forsaken me?" When He said this, He was experiencing your punishment so that you could be part of His family.

  If you have never admitted your sin and recognized your need for a Savior, and you want to become a member of God's family today, then pray this prayer after me:

  Father, thank You that You want me to be a part of Your family. I admit that I am a sinner, and that my sin has come between You and me. I know that I deserve to be separated from You forever. Thank you that Jesus took my punishment on Himself for me. I want to turn away from my sin. I believe that Jesus is Your only Son and that He is fully God and fully man. I receive Him as my Savior and Lord. My life belongs to You. I want to love You and do Your will. Thank You for Your salvation. Thank You that I am now a part of Your "forever family." In Jesus' name, Amen.

  B. Close by encouraging your students to share with their family what they have learned today.
    1. Encourage students who prayed to receive Jesus as their Savior to tell their parents about their decision.
    2. Encourage your students to tell their family about God's desire for a family and to tell them

the stories they learned today.

3. Encourage them to have their parents help them practice saying the five books of the Pentateuch and reciting the main events of Genesis with the hand motions.

4. Remind them about the at-home study pages at Forerunner Kids Club and encourage them to take a few minutes each day to work on them.

5. Give out the Car Talk page for them to give to their parents on the way home.

Questions to jump-start conversation with your 7- to 12-year-old on the way home from church:

1. Who did you learn about in Sunday School today? Were there any families? (Note: We studied Adam and Eve, Cain and Abel, and Noah and his family.)

2. Which was your favorite story? Could you tell it to me?

3. Why did you like this story? What did God speak to you through it?

This week's memory verse: "If you do what is right, will you not be accepted? But if you do not do what is right, sin is crouching at your door; it desires to have you, but you must master it." (Gen. 4:7)

Key thoughts to remember:
1. God created man in His own image because He desired them to be His family.
2. God created man and woman with an innocent spirit and free will. He gave them opportunity to choose between good and evil, between obedience and disobedience.
3. Even though God knew man would choose sin, God already had a plan to restore us to fellowship with Him.

THEME: *The Pentateuch*

Lesson 2: *God's desire for a family*

Day One: Genesis 6

I. Read Genesis chapter 6. As you do, answer the following:

A. In verse 4, God limits man's lifespan to 120 years. Look at chapter 5 to see how long men's lifespans were before this. Notice that chapter 5 is a list of fathers and sons.

B. In verse 5, what do we find out about the hearts of men?

C. How did God feel about this?

D. What did God decide to do?

E. Who found favor in the eyes of the Lord?

F. Verse 9 tells us why he found favor with the Lord. What were three good things about him?

G. Who were Noah's three sons?

H. What did God tell Noah that He was going to do?

I. What did God tell Noah to do?

J. Look at verse 18. How did God say that he would relate to Noah?

II.   Think about these things and write down your thoughts.

A. Why do you think God's heart was filled with pain?

B. God made a covenant with Noah. This means an agreement that brings a relationship of commitment between God and His people. What does this tell you about God's desire to have a family?

C. Think about your lifestyle. Are you living to find favor in God's eyes?

THEME: *The Pentateuch*

Lesson 2: *God's desire for a family*

Day Two: Genesis 7

I. Read Genesis chapter 7. As you do, answer the following:

    A. Look back at Genesis 6:15. What were the dimensions of the ark? Ask your parents to help you figure out how many of your houses could fit in the ark.

    B. Regarding the animals and birds, what did God command Noah to bring in the ark?

    C. What were the two types of animal/bird couples that God named?

    D. How old was Noah when he entered the ark?

    E. Who accompanied him into the ark?

    F. The ark door was *very* big. Who shut it?

    G. For how many days did it rain?

    H. For how long did the waters flood the earth?

II. Think about these things and write down your thoughts.

    A. Because of Noah's righteousness, his family was saved—his wife, his three sons, and their wives. What does this tell you about the importance of family to God?

    B. Do you think that Noah taught his sons about God and led them in a life of worship?

    C. Do you think that his sons listened to him?

    D. What does this tell you about the importance of parents communicating their values and beliefs to their children? And the importance of children listening with respect?

THEME: *The Pentateuch*

Lesson 2: *God's desire for a family*

Day Three: Genesis 8

I. Read Genesis chapter 8. As you do, answer the following:

   A. How does Moses introduce the end of the flood? What does he tell us that God did or thought in 8:1?

   B. Where did the ark land?

   C. Why did Noah send out the raven?

   D. Why did he send out the dove?

   E. What did the dove bring back the second time? What did this tell Noah?

   F. How old was Noah when they left the ark?

   G. Compare this with his age in 7:11, when they entered the ark. How long were they in the ark?

   H. What was the first thing that Noah did when he left the ark?

   I. What promise did God make to mankind after this?

II.   Think about these things and write down your thoughts.

   A. What do you think Noah and his family did during that long year in the ark, other than take care of the animals? What do you think they talked about?

   B. Moses said, "God remembered Noah and the wild animals and the livestock." Do you think that God had forgotten them? Why do you think Moses used the word, "Remembered?" What does that word tell you about the relationship between God and His creation?

   C. Why do you think Noah offered a sacrifice to God?

   D. God promised not to destroy the animals, birds, and humans again in judgment, even though every inclination of man's heart is evil, even from childhood. Does this give you any hint about how God will relate to His creation after the flood? What do you think?

At-Home Daily Activity Sheet 4

THEME: *The Pentateuch*

Lesson 2: *God's desire for a family*

Day Four: Genesis 9

I. Read Genesis 9: 1-19. As you do, answer the following:

 A. What was God's blessing/command to Noah's family in verse 1?

 B. In verse 3, God gives man something new to eat. What is it?

 C. What new punishment does God give them in verses 6?

 D. Remember that a covenant is an agreement that brings about a special relationship between God and His people. What is the covenant that God makes with Noah and his descendents and with every living creature that was represented on the ark?

 E. What is the sign of that covenant?

 F. What does verse 19 tell us about where everyone on the earth came from?

II. Think about these things and write down your thoughts.

 A. When Cain killed Abel, God cursed Cain, but did not require Cain to be put to death. Why do you think God instituted the death penalty after the flood?

 B. What do you think is the importance of God's promise to never destroy the whole world by flood again? Why do you think God would make a promise like that?

 C. The rainbow reminds us of God's promise to us. Read Revelation 4:3. There is a description of what John saw at the throne of God. What did he see? Why do you think it is there?

 D. We've talked about God's desire for a family and that He desires to be a Father to us. What does the story of Noah and his family speak to you about God and His family?

THEME: *The Pentateuch*

Lesson 2: *God's desire for a family*

Day Five: Genesis 11

I. Read Genesis 11. As you do, answer the following:

    A. What was the name of the plain where people settled after the flood?

    B. What two reasons did they give for building the great tower in the city?

        1. Reason one:

        2. Reason two:

    C. Why did the Lord cause new languages to form suddenly?

    D. What did the people do when they began speaking other languages? Where did they go?

    E. What new name did they give the city?

    F. Read verses 10-32. This is a genealogy, a list of ancestors. Some of the names list a father followed by his son; some list a father followed by his great-great-grandson. In the Hebrew language, the relationship-family word can mean "father of" or "ancestor of" so we don't know exactly in each case. Who is the first person listed in this genealogy? Whose names do you find at the end of the genealogy?

    G. Verses 27 –32 tell us about Terah's family.
        1. Who are Terah's sons?

        2. Who is Terah's grandson?

        3. Who are Terah's daughter-in-laws? To whom is each married?

        4. Where were they all born?

        5. They set out on a journey to go where?

        6. Where did they settle instead?

II.   Think about these things and write down your thoughts.

1. Why do you think the Lord cared if the people built a tower to the sky or not?
2. Noah had taught his sons about the one true God. Do you think they passed on these teachings to their sons and grandsons?
3. There are many ancient mythologies. Did the descendants of Noah hold on to the family faith in God?s

First Quarter, Year One: Biblical Foundations for Children
Lesson Three:
Genesis: God Chooses a Man

Objective: To introduce the man, Abraham, whom God chose to make into His special nation because God is a Father who desires a family.

Key verse for this lesson: "Abraham will surely become a great and powerful nation, and all the nations on earth will be blessed through him. *For I have chosen Him*, so that he will direct his children and his household after him to keep the way of the Lord by doing what is right and just, so that the Lord will bring about for Abraham what He has promised him." (Gen. 18:18-19, emphasis added)

Key thoughts to consider and to pass on:
1. God chose Abraham from among hundreds of thousands of people.
2. He chose Abraham because Abraham lived righteously and worshipped the one true God, in the midst of people worshipping false gods and living unrighteously.
3. He blessed Abraham so that all the nations on the earth would be blessed through him. That is, God chose Abraham to be the father of a nation, so that from that nation, 2,000 years later, a child would be born who would be the Savior of the nations.
4. God chose a man and his family so that through that family, God would redeem for himself a family. Through that family, God would restore men and women to Himself, so that He could have a loving, intimate relationship with them. God chose Abraham and his family to be the family for the Bridegroom King, Jesus, who would come to redeem from Himself a Bride, a collective people of God.

Review from last week:

I. The beginning of history
   A. Creation (1:1-2:25)
   B. Fall of Adam and Eve (3:1-24)
   C. Cain and Abel (4:1-26)
   D. Descendants of Adam (5:1-32)
   E. The flood (6:1-9:29)
   F. Genesis of nations (10:1-32)
   G. Tower of Babel (11:1-9)
   H. Genealogy of Abraham (11:10-32)

II. The beginning of the nation of Israel
   A. Abraham (12:1-25:18)
   B. Isaac (25:19-26:35)
   C. Jacob (27:1-36:43)
   D. Joseph (37:1-50:26)

Biblical Foundation

I. Read Genesis chapters 12-22. As you do, journal your answers to the following questions. Because this is an extended passage, you should work on two to three Bible chapters a day so that you have ample time to pray and reflect over the Word.

1. At the start of chapter 12, what does God tell Abram to do?

2. What does God promise to Abram?

3. When Abram gets as far south as Shechem, which is halfway between the Sea of Galilee and the Dead Sea, the Lord appears to him. What does God promise him?

4. After this, he leaves the mountain valley where Shechem is located, and he goes further south to a valley in the hill country. What towns are east and west of him here?

5. What does Abram do when there is famine in the land? To where does he go?

6. After the famine, to where does Abram return? What does he do there?

7. Look at 12:7, 12:8, and 13:3. What do you think is the importance of the altars? Why do you think Abram keeps building them?

8. What causes Abram and Lot to part ways?

9. To where does Lot move and why does he choose it?

10. What does God promise Abram after Lot departs? What part of this promise has Abram heard already? What new information does God give him (or, what else does God promise him)?

11. Abram moves further south. To where does he move? What does he do when he gets there?

12. In chapter 14, we read the tale of the capture and rescue of Lot. The kings in the region of Babylon (the king of Shinar and the king of Elam) have conquered the kings of the city-states of Canaan, and for twelve years they have required the Canaanite cities to pay tribute (taxes). In the thirteenth year, the Canaanite kings refuse to pay, so in the fourteenth year, the kings from the Babylon region march their armies out to enforce the payment.

    This is a common story that happened to the Canaanites and to the Israelites many times over the millennia. Much of the time, the people living in the area between the Jordan River and the Mediterranean Sea were paying tribute to either the Pharaoh/king of Egypt or to the king of Elam/Babylon/Assyria/Persia.

It would be as if there were one or two great powers in South America and one or two in North America, and every time a new king rose to power in one of them, he would rally his troops to challenge the great power south or north of him. Central America would be like Israel—getting trampled down every time the great powers met to fight, and in between wars having to pay tribute to the winner of the last war.

a. When the kings of the East conquer the kings of Sodom and Gomorrah, what happens to Lot?

b. What name is given to Abram in verse 13? _____ This is the first time this term is used in the Bible. It may come from Eber, Abram's ancestor.

c. What does Abram do? How important is family to Abram?

d. With only 318 trained warriors, Abram routs the four kings of the East. What does that tell you about Abram's strategy as a general and about God's favor on him?

e. As he nears home, Abram encounters another city-state's king, who brings him bread and wine (does this remind you of communion elements?). Who is the king and what city does he rule?

f. Notice that although he lives in the midst of the Canaanites who worship many different false gods, Melchizedek, whose name means "Righteous King," worships El Elyon, the Most High God. That is, he worships the one true God. What does he declare about Abram?

g. What does Abram give him?

13. At the close of the chapter, Abram refuses to take any reward in payment for returning everything to Sodom and Gomorrah. What is the response of the Lord to this, in 15:1?

14. What is Abram's response in verses 2 and 3? Why does he feel this way?

15. What does God promise him?

16. What is Abram's response?

At this point, Abram is in his early 80s. Up until now, he has believed God about a number of things. He believed God sent him to Canaan, and when he traveled, he believed that God would lead him to the very spot he was to settle down. He had no children, yet when God promised the land of Canaan to him and his descendents, he believed. Yet here, when God tells him that he will have descendents as numerous as the stars, and he believes, *at this point*, God credits his faith as righteousness. Paul refers to this in Romans 4 (go ahead and read that chapter). He uses this to demonstrate that salvation comes by believing God alone, and not by actions of obedience to the law.

This is why God chose Abram to be the head of the family line from whom Jesus would come—because Abram was a man of faith.

17. So Abram believes that God will give him physical descendents, but he asks for reassurance that he and his family will gain possession of Canaan. So God makes a covenant with Abram, a promise which God himself pledged to keep.

    a. What animals does God command Abram to bring?

    b. What does Abram do with them?

    c. Who (or what, representing whom) passes between them?

This is an ancient form of covenant making. If it were a dependent covenant, where each party had to do something in order to assure the outcome, then each would walk between the pieces. If it were an independent covenant, where one party was pledging to do something for the other party, regardless of the actions of the second party, then the pledging party alone passed between the pieces. So here God is pledging an unconditional promise to Abram.

18. What does God prophesy about Abram's descendents and the land? What will happen?

19. Why won't Abram's children and grandchildren inherit the land right away?

20. What two borders does God promise to Abram?

21. So God has been talking to Abram about his descendents. Why does Sarai give Hagar to Abram?

Note: this was an ancient custom. If the wife could not bear children, then the wife's servant would bear the child fathered by the wife's husband, and the wife would be present at delivery to claim the child as her own. Usually then the wife raised the child as her own, as if she had born him.

Does Abram consult the Lord about Sarai's idea?

22. What happens to Hagar's attitude when she discovers she is pregnant?

23. Whom does Sarai blame?

24. What does Abram do?

25. What does Sarai do?

26. What does the angel of the Lord tell Hagar to do?

27. What does he promise Hagar about her baby?

Note: the Arabs, particularly Mohammed of Islam, trace their heritage through Ishmael.

28. What happens when Abram is 99 years old?

Note: The last time God spoke with Abram was thirteen years earlier. Even though it appears that God is always appearing to Abram, often many years separate each appearance.

29. Why does God appear to Abram at this time?

30. Why does God change his name to Abraham?

Note: Name changes are important in the Bible, indicating a change in heart or a change in position. Abram to Abraham, Jacob (the deceiver) to Israel (prince with God), Simon to Peter, Saul to Paul, etc.

31. What physical act does God give Abraham to perform as a sign of the covenant between God and Abraham's family line?

32. What is the basis for Abraham's salvation? Circumcision or faith?

33. What is Sarai's name change, and what promise goes along with it?

34. What promise did God give Abraham concerning Ishmael?

35. Based on Abraham's heart for Ishmael, how do you think he felt about the boy? In the New Testament we read about Ishmael as the son of the bondwoman, the human-works baby, as opposed to Isaac, the faith-baby, the promised child. Do you think Abraham thought of Ishmael like that? Or did Abraham have a true father's heart full of love for his son? After all, for 14 years, Ishmael was Abraham's only son.

36. How long did Abraham take to fulfill God's command of circumcision from the time that God gave it to him?

37. At the start of chapter 18, God appears to Abraham again. This time it is only a few months since God last appeared to him. Describe the scene as God appears:

38. Sarah bakes bread, and the servants slaughter and prepare a young calf. How long do you

think it takes for them to prepare this meal? What do you think Abraham and his guests are doing while the cooking is going on?

39. During their meal, what does God tell Abraham about him and Sarah?

40. What is Sarah's response? What had Abraham's response been, a few months back in Gen. 17:17?

Is there any wonder, then, that God told them to name the baby, Isaac, which means "laughing" or "laughter" or "he laughs"?

41. Does Sarah have the same intimate relationship with God that Abraham does? Look at verse 15. What kind of a relationship does Sarah have with God?

Imagine that you are surrounded with people who worship spirits whom they consider to be gods, which are represented by statutes made in shapes of part animal/part human forms, or formed like several animals together. And you worship a God who visits you or visits your husband from time to time in the form of a human man, and yet has power to appear and disappear, to make things happen, to promise impossible things and fulfill those promises; you also know about Him from stories passed down from your ancestors.

    a. If you were Abraham, and you had spoken face to face with Him, how would you feel about Him?

    b. If you were Sarah, and you had only heard about Him from your husband and from watching what He told your husband to do, how would you feel about Him?

42. Why does God choose to share with Abraham what is about to happen to Sodom and Gomorrah?

43. Describe Abraham's intercession for the cities.

44. Abraham stops at ten righteous people. He knows that Lot, Lot's wife, and Lot's two daughters live in Sodom. That makes four people. Then the two young men who were the fiancés of the girls. That makes six. Do you think Abraham was hoping that Lot had influenced a few people in the city, perhaps one other family, and led them to worship the one true God?

45. What time do the angels arrive at Sodom and where is Lot sitting?

When we read that Lot was sitting at the city gate, this means that he is in a position of authority in Sodom. This is where the city elders would sit to hear legal cases and make decisions.

46. Why do you think Lot insisted that the two men (who were really angels) stay at his house? Is Lot aware of the rampant sin in the city?

47. How do you think Lot's daughters felt when Lot offered them to the crowd of men?

48. What does this tell you about the value of women in those days?

49. How do the men of Sodom respond to Lot? What does this tell you about their moral condition?

50. How do the angels intervene to save Lot?

51. The angels tell Lot to gather any other family members to flee the city because judgment is coming. How do Lot's future sons-in-laws respond? What does this tell you about Lot's influence over them, specifically: has he convinced them to worship the one true God?

52. How easily do Lot and his family leave the city? How do the angels help them?

53. Remember that at this point, Abraham is 99 years old, and Lot is maybe 25 or 30 years younger than he, 50 years younger at the most. He's at least 50, maybe older. So Lot says, "I'll never make it to the mountains! How about that little village that's partway to the mountains? I think I can make it there." The angel accedes to his request. It takes him from sunrise (about 6:00am) until the sun has risen over the whole land—maybe 8:00 or 9:00am— for him to get to Zoar. And then burning sulfur comes from the heavens down upon Sodom and Gomorrah.

We read that Lot's wife looked back and became a pillar of salt. Luke 17:31-32 gives us a little insight into what happened to her. It was more than a matter of looking from curiosity. Jesus says, "On that day . . . no one in the field should go back for anything. Remember Lot's wife!" This is set in a passage about the last days, when Jesus returns. He goes on to say, "Whoever tries to keep his life will lose it" (Lk. 17:33). So it appears that Lot's wife did more than just look back; she went back. Perhaps she remembered something that she wanted to have brought with her, something she didn't want to lose. In the process of going back to get it, she got caught in the downpour of burning sulfur and became, as it were, a pillar of salt. What do you think about this?

54. In verse 29, why did God deliver Lot? Do you think that God would have delivered Lot, had Abraham not interceded with the Lord?

55. Genesis 19:37-38: Lot's oldest daughter has a son by her father. What is his name and what nation comes from him? Lot's youngest daughter? Notice that from this sinful situation come two of Israel's greatest nation-enemies. Indeed, the present-day city of Amman, Jordan, is the original capital of the Ammonite nation. It has been the city of Amman ever since the Ammonites lived there.

56. Genesis 20:1: Where does Abraham move?

57. Who is the city-king?

Note: This is not actually his name, no more than Pharaoh was the actual name of each king of Egypt. It is a title and means "high king" or "father king."

58. In the custom of that day, if a king wanted to insure peace between himself and another king or a very important man who had much wealth and many servants, he required that a marriage take place between one of his children and one of the other king's children. In this case, Abraham had no children. Who does Abimelech take as the "peace-maker?"

59. How does Abimelech find out that Sarah is not only Abraham's sister, but also his wife?

60. What kind of a dream is this? Is it the type that requires interpretation?

61. How does Abraham explain why he said that Sarah was his sister?

62. How does Abimelech rectify the situation?

63. So Sarah returns to Abraham, and what happens next with them? What does Abraham name this son?

64. When Isaac is 8 days old, what does Abraham do with him? Thus Isaac enters into the covenant that God made with Abraham.

65. When Isaac is about 2 or 3 years old, Abraham has a party for him. By this time Ishmael is about 16 or 17 years old, and is playing the part of "big brother." Up until Isaac's birth, Ishmael had been Abraham's sole heir. Now Isaac is 2 or 3 years old, and this party is celebrating the fact that he has lived through those early few years when infant mortality was pretty high. Suddenly Ishmael has real competition for that inheritance, and as the son of the wife of Abraham, not the son of his concubine, Isaac stands to inherit the bulk of Abraham's goods and flocks. So what does Ishmael do at the party?

66. When Sarah sees, how does she respond?

67. How does Abraham feel about this? How does he feel about Ishmael?

68. What does God promise Abraham concerning Ishmael?

69. What does Abraham do early the next morning?

70. How do you think Hagar feels? After all, this is the second time she finds herself in the

desert because of Ishmael.

71. When they run out of water, do you think she remembers the prophetic word that the angel of the Lord gave her about her son the last time she was in the desert? Or is she in despair?

72. What does an angel tell her this time?

73. So where do they live, and whom does Ishmael marry?

74. Why does Abimelech want to make a covenant or treaty with Abraham?

75. There is a well in dispute between Abraham and the servants of Abimelech. This becomes the site of the covenant-making between Abraham and Abimelech. What does Abraham give Abimelech in pledge of his honesty?

76. What do they name the well?

Note: A city grows up near the well and takes its name from the well. The city, named Beersheva, is there to this day.

77. Once Abraham's ownership of this well has been secured, what does Abraham do there?

78. In Genesis 22:1, we read that God was testing Abraham when He sent him to sacrifice Isaac. What do you think that God was testing in Abraham? His commitment to God? His faith in the promise concerning Isaac? Read Hebrews 11:17-19.

79. In those days, people often offered their children in sacrifice to their gods. Do you think Abraham was surprised that God was requiring the sacrifice of his child?

80. In verse 5, what does Abraham tell the servants? What does this say about what he believes will happen?

81. When Isaac asks about the lamb, what does Abraham reply to him?

82. How do you think Isaac felt when his father bound him and put him on the altar?

83. What does God say to Abraham through the angel of the Lord?

84. What does Abraham find to sacrifice?

85. How do you think Isaac felt when the ram was being sacrificed?

86. After the sacrifice is made, what does the angel of the Lord communicate to Abraham?

87. At the close of this chapter, what do we learn about Abraham's family?

II. Look back over Genesis 12-22

    A. Write down the verse references and a short summary of each of the promises to Abraham and the Abrahamic covenant:

    B. Write a short summary of the story of Ishmael.

C. Write a short summary of the story of Isaac.

III. Reflect upon the following:

A. Through this study, what has God spoken to you about:

1. His emotions:

2. His feelings and desires concerning a family of His own, particularly relating to the choosing of Abraham and his family:

3. His eternal purposes:

B. Finish these sentences:

1. When I read about the promise of God to Abram, I thought . . .

2. I believe God chose Abram because . . .

 And it was a good choice because . . .

3. As I read through the story of Abraham, I noticed he made a number of mistakes, like . . .

4. Even though Abraham kept making mistakes, I noticed that God . . .

5. Through God's choosing of one man and one family to become His chosen people, His chosen nation, God spoke to me about . . .

IV. Map Time

Locate the following cities:
1. Ur: the city where Abram was born.
2. Haran: the city to which he and his family traveled; his father, Terah, died here. From here Abram sets out to go to the land which God would show him.
3. Jerusalem: where Abraham was willing to sacrifice Isaac.
4. Hebron: where Abraham lived, under the oaks of Mamre (on the map below, it would be under Jerusalem, about 1/3 of the way down the Dead Sea.

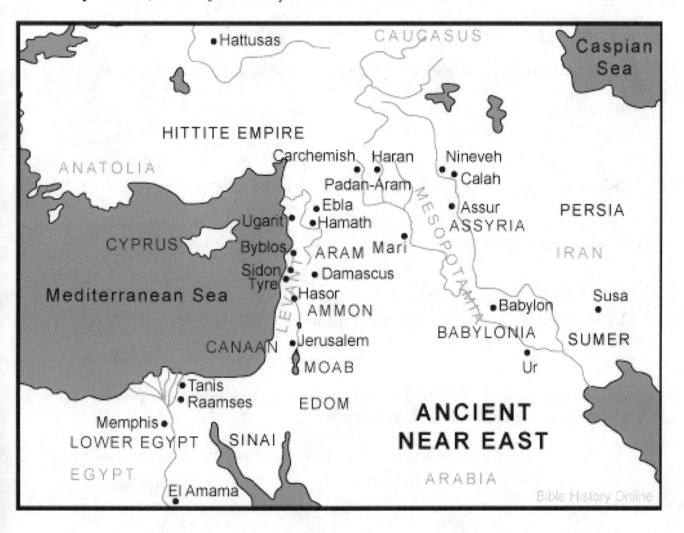

THEME: *The Pentateuch*
Lesson 2: *Genesis: God chooses a man*

Part One: The Invitation

A. Review the unit theme.
    1. Unit theme:

    2. Lead your students in reciting the names of the five books of the Pentateuch.

    3. Lead your students in reciting the main events of Genesis, with hand motions:

Creation	Abraham
Fall	Isaac
Flood	Jacob
Tower of Babel	Joseph
Nations scatter	To Egypt

B. Introduce today's lesson topic and explain why God chose a man to become a chosen nation from whom would come the Messiah.

C. Ask the students what they remember about the words, "God is a family man." Have several students share their thoughts.

D. Share with your students what you feel about God choosing a man and entering into relationship with that man and his family forever.

    1. The fact that God looked over the earth and chose Abraham excites me because . . .

    2. When I think about the truth that God chooses people, and I think about Him choosing me, I feel . . .

E. Invite your students to meet with God and His desire for them through His choosing of Abraham.

Part Two: The Impartation

I. Things to consider as you prepare:
  A. Through the story of Abraham, what jumped out at you concerning what God wants you to share with your students?
    1. You might trace the theme of God's promises to Abraham.
    2. You might introduce God's overall promises to and covenant with Abraham, then focus on one aspect of it. For example, you might show how God began fulfilling the promises through the birth and life of Isaac.

  B. There are various methods of presentation.
    1. You might use storytelling: telling the story in a dramatic tone of voice, using gestures.
      a. You might focus on the main points of Abraham's story, weaving it into one story, then bring out teaching points.
      b. You might use several of the stories. As you tell the stories, go one by one and after each story bring out a main teaching point or two related to the theme of God's choice of Abraham.

    2. You might use drama.
      a. Act out God making the covenant with Abraham. You be "God" and have one of the students be Abraham. While you give him instructions, have him act out cutting the animals in halves and laying them out. Then you walk between "the animal parts" and proclaim the covenant.
      b. Break into small groups and give each a story:
        1. God and the two angels visit Abraham and Sarah and promise that Abraham and Sarah will have a son the next year, Isaac. Include Abraham interceding for Sodom.
        2. Ishmael teasing Isaac and being sent away with his mother. Include Sarah talking to Abraham about it, God talking to Abraham about it and the promise regarding Ishmael, and the angel of the Lord talking to Hagar.
        3. The sacrifice of Isaac.

    3. You might use a mix of the two, where you tell the story, but you have students act it out in front of the others as you tell the story and direct them into their places.

II. Preparing the Impartation Segment:

    1. The method I will use:

    2. The story/stories I will use:

II. The Impartation

As you begin the first story about Abram/Abraham, put up his picture on the time line, at the year 2000 B.C.

Next, use your map of the ancient Middle East to show your students the location of Ur, Haran, Hebron, and Jerusalem.

    A. First story

        1. Telling the story:

        2. Truths to which I will draw my students' attention:

    B. Second story

        1. Telling the story:

        2. Truths to which I will draw my students' attention:

C. Third story

1. Telling the story:

2. Truths to which I will draw my students' attention.

Part Three: The Application

Ask the students to write answers to the following questions in their journals.

1. Why do you think God chose Abraham?

2. God often works through one person. He used one man, Noah, to save a remnant of the human race to begin the world over again after the flood. He used one man, Abraham, to begin his chosen people, from whom would come Jesus. And He used one man, one God-man, Jesus, to save the people of the world from their sins and redeem them to God. When God chose Noah and Abraham, what were His criteria? What was God looking for? How can you be someone whom God can use to fulfill His purposes on the earth?

3. Listen to what God says to us through the Apostle Peter in I Peter 2:9, "*You* (you believers in Jesus), you are a chosen people, a royal priesthood, a holy nation, a people belonging to God *so that* you may declare the praises of Him who called you out of darkness into his wonderful light" (emphasis and comment added). God chose Abraham so that his children would be God's chosen people and a holy nation. The Apostle Paul, in the book of Romans, tells us that when we put our faith in Jesus, when we believe that Jesus took the penalty for our sins, then we are grafted into the nation of Israel, into the people of God. So you are part of God's chosen people.

How does it make you feel to know that you are chosen by God? How can you declare His praises?

Depending on which story/stories you used in your lesson, select a few questions from the questions you answered in the Biblical Foundation section.

Additional questions:

Part Four: The Impact

A. Explain to your students that Abraham was justified by his faith. A simple way to understand what it means to be justified before God is that when God makes me justified, it is just as if I'd never sinned. God makes me righteous in His sight. Abraham believed God would do what God promised, and this made Abraham righteous in the sight of God. When we believe that Jesus is fully God and fully man, and that He died to take the punishment for our sins, then we are justified by our faith.

The Apostle James also taught us that faith which is not walked out by proper action is dead faith; it has no life (Jas. 2:17). When we place our faith in Jesus, He will give us power to conquer the sin in our life and live according to his law of love. The Apostle John told us that when we love one another, when our actions are motivated by love for one another, then we know we have passed from spiritual death to spiritual life (1 Jn. 3:4).

Invite your students to make a commitment to living out their faith daily by using God's grace to overcome sin and by choosing to do and say things guided by love for others. Invite them to pray this after you:

Father, thank You that You have chosen me to be a part of Your family. I believe You. Jesus, I believe that You are fully God and fully man, and that You love me completely. I trust what You are doing in my life. You are the best leader, and I believe that You work everything together for good in my life.

Father, I want to walk out my faith. Just like Abraham believed You, so he left his nation and kept traveling until You told him, "This is the place I am giving you," I want to live a life of faith. Give me grace to overcome sin in my life. Give me grace to love my family, to love my friends, and to love my enemies. Teach me how to love them well. I believe that just as You have chosen me and saved me, You will also sanctify me—You will help me to live a holy life. I want to live a life that brings praise to Your Name through the name of Jesus, Amen.

B. Close by encouraging your students to share with their family what they have learned today.
    1. Encourage students who prayed to receive Jesus as their Savior to tell their parents about their decision.
    2. Encourage your students to tell their family about how God chose Abraham and made his family into a chosen nation. Encourage them to tell their family the stories they learned today.
    3. Encourage them to have their parents help them practice saying the five books of the Pentateuch and reciting the main events of Genesis with the hand motions.
    4. Remind them about the at-home study pages at Forerunner Kids Club and encourage them to take a few minutes each day to work on them.
    5. Give out the Car Talk page.

Questions to jump-start conversation with your 7- to 12-year-old on the way home from church:

1. So tell me about Abraham. Why did God choose Abraham?

2. Can you tell me a story about Abraham?

3. Why did you like this story? What did God speak to you through it?

This week's Memory Verse:

"Abraham will surely become a great and powerful nation, and all the nations on earth will be blessed through him. *For I have chosen him*, so that he will direct his children and his household after him to keep the way of the Lord by doing what is right and just, so that the Lord will bring about for Abraham what He has promised him." (Gen. 18:18-19, emphasis added)

Key thoughts to remember:
1. God chose Abraham from among hundreds of thousands of people.
2. He chose Abraham because Abraham lived righteously and worshipped the one True God, in the midst of people worshipping false gods and living unrighteously.
3. He blessed Abraham so that all the nations on the earth would be blessed through him. That is, God chose Abraham to be the father of a nation, so that from that nation, 2,000 years later, a child would be born who would be the Savior of the nations.
4. God chose a man and his family so that through that family, God would redeem for himself a family. Through that family, God would restore men and women to Himself, so that He could have a loving, intimate relationship with them. God chose Abraham and his family to be the family for the Bridegroom King, Jesus, who would come to redeem from Himself a Bride, a collective people of God.

THEME: *The Pentateuch*

Lesson 3: *God chooses a man, Abraham*

Day One: Genesis 12

I. Read Genesis chapter 12. As you do, answer the following:

   In verse 1, what is God's command to Abraham?

   2. In verses 2-3, God promises Abram many things. What are they?
   I will make you into _____
   I will bless_____
   I will make _____
   You will be _____
   Those who bless you, I will _____
   Those who curse you, I will _____
   All peoples on earth _____

   3. How would God bless all peoples on the earth through Abraham?

   4. How old was Abram when he left on this journey?

   5. Who went with him?

   6. When he arrived at Shechem, what did he do?

   7. What did God say to him there?

   8. Where did he move next?

   9. What did he build there?

II.   Think about these things and write down your thoughts.

   1. Why do you think God chose Abram and made many promises to him?

   2. Why do you think God wanted to bless all the people of the earth?

THEME: *The Pentateuch*

Lesson 3: *God chooses a man, Abraham*

Day Two: Genesis 15

I. Read Genesis chapter 15. As you do, answer the following:

1. What was Abram's concern at the start of the chapter?

2. Where does God take Abram?

3. What does God promise him?

4. How does Abram respond?

5. In verse 7, what does God promise Abram next?

6. What animals does God tell Abram to prepare?

7. God walks between these animal and pledges an unconditional covenant with Abram. This mean God will keep His promise no matter what.

8. What does God prophesy will happen to Abram's descendants?

II.   Think about these things and write down your thoughts.

1. How do you think Abraham felt when God appeared to him again to talk about the covenant?

2. Look at verse 18. Why do you think modern-day Israelis (who are the physical descendants of Abraham) believe that the land of Israel belongs to them alone? What do you think?

THEME: *The Pentateuch*

Lesson 3: *God chooses a man, Abraham*

Day Three: Genesis 17

I. Read Genesis chapter 17. As you do, answer the following:

  1. What happened when Abram was 99 years old?

  2. Why did God change Abram's name? What was his new name?

  3. What promises did God make to Abraham?

  4. What did God tell Abraham to do as a sign of the covenant between God and Abraham's descendants?

  5. What was Sarai's new name?

  6. What was Abraham's first reaction to the thought of old Sarah having a baby?

  7. What did God tell Abraham to name this baby?

  8. What about Ishmael? What would God do about him?

II.   Think about these things and write down your thoughts.

  1. Abraham was living in the middle of many idol worshippers. How do you think he felt when his God kept appearing to him and talking to him?

  2. How was Abraham's relationship with God different from the relationship that the Canaanites had with their gods?

THEME: *The Pentateuch*

Lesson 3: *God chooses a man, Abraham*

Day Four: Genesis 18

I. Read Genesis 18. As you do, answer the following:

1. Abraham was sitting in the doorway of his tent-house in the early afternoon. Whom did he see walking toward him?

2. Look at his words to them in verses 3 and 4. Does Abraham know who it is?

3. What does he tell Sarah to do?

4. What other food does he have prepared for them to eat?

5. What does God say will happen in the next year for Abraham and Sarah?

6. Is Sarah listening? What does she think of this?

7. What does God tell Abraham about the cities of Sodom and Gomorrah?

8. What is Abraham's response?

9. What number of righteous people does he begin with? At what number does he stop?

II.   Think about these things and write down your thoughts.

1. God had appeared to Abraham several times before, in dreams and in person. How do you think Abraham felt about God walking up to his house, accompanied by two men (angels)?

2. What do you think about people preparing a meal for God to sit down and eat?

3. Remember that his nephew, Lot, lived in Sodom at that time. Lot, his wife, his two daughters and their fiancés. That makes six people. Why do you think Abraham stopped at ten righteous people?

4. If you knew that God were going to destroy a nearby city, would you intercede for the people of that city? Do you intercede for the unsaved people of your town or city?

At-Home Daily Activity Sheet 5

THEME: *The Pentateuch*

Lesson 3: *God chooses a man, Abraham*

Day Five: Genesis 19 (the story of Lot)

I. Read Genesis 19. As you do, answer the following:

1. Where was Lot sitting when the two angels arrived at the city? This means that Lot was a city official.

2. What does he insist that they do?

3. What do the angels ask Lot in verse 12?

4. Do they find ten righteous people in Sodom?

5. What do the angels do with Lot and his family at dawn?

6. What happens to Sodom and Gomorrah?

7. What does Lot's wife do?

II.   Think about these things and write down your thoughts.

1. Genesis 13:10-11 says that Lot chose to live in the plains near the Jordan River because it was lush pastureland for his flocks. He chose that and left the desert area to his uncle Abraham. We don't know why Lot chose to live in the city of Sodom instead of living in tents near his flock, like Abraham did. What do you think about Lot's choice?

2. We read that Lot's wife looked back and became a pillar of salt. Luke 17:31-32 gives us a little insight into what happened to her. It was more than a matter of looking from curiosity. Jesus says, "On that day . . . no one in the field should go back for anything. Remember Lot's wife!" This is set in a passage about the last days, when Jesus returns. He goes on to say, "Whoever tries to keep his life will lose it" (Lk. 17:33). So it appears that Lot's wife did more than just look back; she went back. Perhaps she remembered something that she wanted to have brought with her, something she didn't want to lose. And in the process of going back to get it, she got caught in the downpour of burning sulfur and became, as it were, a pillar of salt. What do you think about this?

THEME: *The Pentateuch*

Lesson 3: *God chooses a man, Abraham*

Day Five: Genesis 22

I. Read Genesis 22. As you do, answer the following:

1.   What did God tell Abraham to do?

2.   How long did it take to get to the mountain?

3.   Whom did Abraham take with him?

4.   Who went up the mountain?

5.   What did Abraham tell the servants?

6.   On the way up the mountain, what did Isaac ask his father?

7.   What did Abraham reply?

8.   What happened when Abraham took the knife to sacrifice his son?

9.   What did Abraham find to sacrifice instead?

10. What does the angel re-affirm to Abraham as a message from God?

II.   Think about these things and write down your thoughts.

1.   Since God had told Abraham to sacrifice his son, why do you think Abraham told the servants that he and his son would worship and come back to them? Look at Hebrews 11:17-19 for a hint.

2.   When Isaac asked where the lamb was, and Abraham replied that God would provide, do you think that Abraham really believed that?

3.   In verse 1, we read that God tested Abraham. In verse 12 He says, "Now I know that you fear God." Then in verse 15 God says that because Abraham was willing to sacrifice his only son (through whom the promise would come), then God would swear by Himself to fulfill the promise. Do you think God needed to test Abraham to know Abraham's heart, or was God revealing Abraham's heart to himself and to future generations so that *we* would know what was in Abraham's heart?

First Quarter, Year One: Biblical Foundations for Children
Lesson Four:
Genesis: Joseph—God planned it for good

Objective: To demonstrate how God used Joseph to preserve the family whom God desired.

Key verse for this lesson: "You intended to harm me, but God intended it for good to accomplish what is now being done: the saving of many lives." (Gen. 50:20)

Key thoughts to consider and to pass on:
1. From the start, God planned to use Joseph to save his entire family during the famine.
2. Joseph's destiny in God was to be a leader and in authority above his brothers. No matter what they did to him, they could not change his destiny in God.
3. Even though Joseph's circumstances changed drastically during various periods of his life, they did not change his destiny.
4. What was most important to Joseph's destiny was his correct response in every season of his life.

Review from last week:

I. The beginning of history
    A. Creation (1:1-2:25)
    B. Fall of Adam and Eve (3:1-24)
    C. Cain and Abel (4:1-26)
    D. Descendants of Adam (5:1-32)
    E. The flood (6:1-9:29)
    F. Genesis of nations (10:1-32)
    G. Tower of Babel (11:1-9)
    H. Genealogy of Abraham (11:10-32)

II. The beginning of the nation of Israel
    A. Abraham (12:1-25:18)
    B. Isaac (25:19-26:35)
    C. Jacob (27:1-36:43)

Biblical Foundation

I. Start at Genesis chapter 37. We're going to skip some chapters in our journaling, but you can read the entire passage from ch. 37-50, if you'd like. Because this is an extended passage, you should work on two to three Bible chapters a day so that you have ample time to pray and reflect over the Word.

    1. Look at Genesis 30:22-24. Notice that Joseph was born to Rachel, Jacob's favorite wife, only after

---

10 other sons had been born to Jacob through Leah, Leah's maid, and Rachel's maid. Remember that Rachel was the only wife whom Jacob wanted, and she had finally bore him a child, a son. So how do you think Jacob felt about Joseph?

2. In Genesis 37:2, what do we learn about his relationship with his brothers?

3. How about his relationship with his father?

4. How did his brothers feel about him?

5. What was his first dream?

6. Did he keep it private and pray over it? What did he do?

7. What was his second dream?

8. How did his father respond?

9. How did his brothers respond?

10. What happened when his father sent him to check on his brothers? What did they plan?

11. Who wanted to rescue him?

12. What did Judah suggest the brothers do with Joseph?

13. How did the brothers present Joseph's disappearance to Jacob?

14. Note: in verses 3 and 12, when Jacob interacts directly with Joseph, God inspires Moses (the writer) to use Jacob's covenant-promise name, "Israel." Then when the brothers tell their lie to their father to deceive him, God inspires Moses to use his given name, "Jacob," which means "deceiver."

15. What did the merchants do with Joseph?

16. In light of his previous dreams, how do you think Joseph feels now?

17. Skip to chapter 39. Where is Joseph and what is he doing?

18. How well is he doing it? Why?

19. What does Potiphar's wife think about Joseph?

20. What is Joseph's response?

21. Against whom did he think he would be sinning?

22. How does Potiphar's wife resolve this?

23. Where does Joseph end up?

24. In the light of the dreams he had had, how do you think he felt when he wound up in prison?

25. Twice now Joseph has suffered a great setback on his way to his destiny. In fact, twice he is betrayed. Does he let it embitter him? At this point, is he feeling sorry for himself? Is he moping around, all depressed? Has he given up? How does he act in the prison?

26. In chapter 40, who joins Joseph in the prison?

27. What are their dreams? How does Joseph interpret them?

28. Do you think this led Joseph to remember his own dreams? How do you think he felt?

29. How do you think Joseph could be so sure of his interpretation of their dreams, given the fact that his dreams had never come true?

30. The cupbearer is restored to his position, but forgets about Joseph. Two whole years go by. How do you think Joseph felt about this? How do you think he handled his disappointment? Here he is not betrayed; he is forgotten, abandoned.

31. Pharaoh has two dreams that no one can interpret. What happens?

32. How long do you think it took for Joseph to get from the prison to the throne room?

33. When Joseph gives Pharaoh a plan to prepare for the famine, do you think he expected to be put in charge?

34. If you were Joseph, and you had experienced so many reversals and betrayals, how would you feel as you began your work as Pharaoh's right-hand man?

35. Look at Genesis 41:46. How old is Joseph when this happens? Chapter 37 told us that he was seventeen when he had those dreams of future leadership. It's been a hard thirteen years: slavery, prison, alone in a foreign land of idol-worshippers. Yet in Genesis 41:16 we see that Joseph has not lost his faith in the one true God and is even willing to take a public stand on his belief. Note that at home in Canaan, his family was the only family worshipping the one true God in the midst of idol worshippers. How strong was Joseph's faith to have survived thirteen years of solitude and difficult circumstances? Isaac was still alive when Joseph was a young man (in fact, Isaac didn't die until Joseph had spent many years in Egypt). As the honored son who didn't have to work as much, do you think Joseph spent many hours at the feet of Isaac, learning the stories of the true God?

36. Read all of chapter 42. How do you think Joseph felt when he saw his brothers? It had been over twenty years since he had seen them last. His last look at them had been a pleading one: "Don't sell me to these strangers!"

37. How does Joseph treat his brothers? What does this tell you about the choices that Joseph had made in his heart? Did he harbor resentment, unforgiveness, or anger? Did he want revenge? Or is he testing them to see if their hearts have changed? What had Joseph chosen to do with the emotions of his heart?

38. Do you think this is one reason why God chose Joseph—because He knew that Joseph would guard his heart and stay true to the Lord? From what you have read about the other brothers, could any of them have done what Joseph did?

39. Compare Genesis 42:37 with 43:8-9. Notice that Reuben first offers his sons as assurance for Benjamin's safety, and Reuben was the one who had planned, in ch. 37, to rescue Joseph. Then, when it is clear that they must return to Egypt to buy more grain, Judah offers his own life as surety for Benjamin's, and it had been Judah's idea in ch. 37 to sell Joseph rather than kill him. Remember that as Jacob's firstborn from Leah, Reuben had more to lose because of the sons of Rachel—Joseph and Benjamin. Without them, Reuben would inherit a double portion. But with one or the other of them alive, Jacob would give the double portion to them, since he loved Rachel first. Yet Reuben loves his father so much that he will give up what benefits himself for what blesses his father.

40. In the first situation, Judah views selling Joseph as more profitable than killing him. He is not motivated by familial love, as is Reuben; he is profit-minded. In the second situation, he is practical-minded. He doesn't believe that any harm will come to Benjamin, and they will all die without food, so he offers himself in pledge for Benjamin's life. Yet in both situations, Judah is clearly a leader in the family.

41. Read ch. 43.

    a. How does Joseph first treat his brothers when they return to Egypt?

    b. Why do you think he didn't reveal himself to them right away?

    c. In verse 8-9, notice it is Judah who pledges himself as surety for Benjamin. Remember it was Judah's idea to sell Joseph.

42. Read ch. 44. Why do you think Joseph set up this situation? Was he testing his brothers? Was he looking to see if they would protect Benjamin?

43. Judah stepped in to offer himself in exchange, just as he had promised his father. Imagine you are Joseph, talking face to face with your half-brother who sold you into slavery some twenty-two years

before. What do you think you are feeling? Then he offers himself to be your slave so that your little brother can go free. Do you think Joseph was tempted to give Judah a taste of his own medicine? Maybe let Judah be a slave until the next time the brothers show up to buy food? How do you think Joseph is feeling?

44. Read ch. 45. Now you know how Joseph felt. He was full of love and compassion towards his brothers. But how did his brothers feel when they learned that this man of power in Egypt, second only to Pharaoh himself, was their brother whom they had sold into slavery? Look at verse 3.

45. Look at verses 5-11. How does Joseph re-interpret their horrible deed to them? Can you believe this—Joseph tells them, "Don't be angry at yourself for selling me here!" Why might they be angry with themselves for having sold him? Probably only if he were to revenge himself. So Joseph is saying, "Don't worry; I'm not out for vengeance."

46. Look at verse 5. Joseph says, "It was to save lives that God sent me here ahead of you." Again, in verse 7 he says, "God sent me ahead of you to preserve for you a remnant on the earth and to save your lives by a great deliverance."

    a. So Joseph sees himself as a forerunner, one sent ahead of the others. Consider how a forerunner not only goes out in advance, but often suffers great personal loss to fulfill his role. What losses did Joseph suffer? What losses did John the Baptist suffer?

    b. Do you think that during his years in prison or as a slave that Joseph understood his role as a forerunner? Probably not. Probably not until he saw his brothers the first time did he understand the role he was to play in saving their lives and in saving their destiny as the people of God.

    c. How would understanding these truths about forerunners help us as forerunners in the last days?

47. Consider verse 11. To these brothers who sold him into slavery and caused so much suffering in his life, Joseph says, "I will provide for you." What does this teach us about holding a spirit of offense against those who wrong us?

48. If you want, you can read ch. 46-49. If not, skip to chapter 50. Jacob lived 17 years in Egypt before he died there. Now look at Gen. 50:15-21. Even after 17 years of living under Joseph's protection, his brothers don't really know his heart towards them. Once Dad is dead, the brothers fear that Joseph will get his revenge for what they did almost 40 years before. So they make up a message for Joseph that they attribute to Jacob. Given all the time that Joseph had privately with Jacob before he died, Joseph knows that if his dad had wanted to communicate this to him, his dad would have said it himself. So in verse 17, what is Joseph's response to their fake message?

49. Look at his words to his brothers in verse 19-21. They still don't understand Joseph's destiny, do they? But Joseph does. He sums it up in verse 20: You intended to harm me, but God intended it

for good, to save many lives. Joseph fully forgave them years and years before, and he rests, un-offended, in his destiny in God. How can this help you as you walk in your destiny before God? Can anyone keep you from fulfilling your destiny? Can any circumstance keep you from fulfilling your destiny? What response does God require of us in any situation?

II. Look back over Genesis 37-50

A. Write a short summary of Joseph's early life, before he was sold, up to his arrival in Egypt. Include his dreams.

B. Write a short summary of Joseph's time at Potiphar's house.

C. Write a short summary of the time Joseph spent in jail. Include the dreams of the baker and cupbearer.

D. Write a short summary of Joseph's encounter with Pharaoh. Include the dreams and interpretation, and Joseph's plan.

E. Write a short summary of Joseph's encounters with his brothers, from the first encounter through their last conversation after Jacob's death.

III. Reflect upon the following:

   A. Through this study, what has God spoken to you concerning:

      1. His emotions:

      2. His feelings and desires concerning a family of His own, particularly relating to the preservation of the line from whom Messiah would come:

3. His eternal purposes:

B. Finish these sentences:

1. When I read about Joseph's brothers plotting to kill him, then selling him into slavery, I thought . . .

2. I believe God chose Joseph because . . .

And it was a good choice because . . .

3. Each time Joseph encountered another setback, I noticed he . . .

4. What I learned through Joseph's responses was . . .

5. Through God's choosing of Joseph and bringing about his destiny no matter what happened to him, God spoke to me about . . .

IV. Map Time

For the life of Joseph, note that he was born in Padan-aram (near Haran) when his father, Jacob, was was working for his uncle Laban. While he was still young, his father moved his family back to Canaan. First they lived in Shechem. On the map below, it's near the unmarked dot above Jerusalem. Then they moved to Isaac's home in Hebron. When Joseph goes to check on his brothers, he goes first to Shechem, then finds they have moved north to Dothan. It is near Dothan that his brothers sell him as a slave. He then is taken to Egypt.

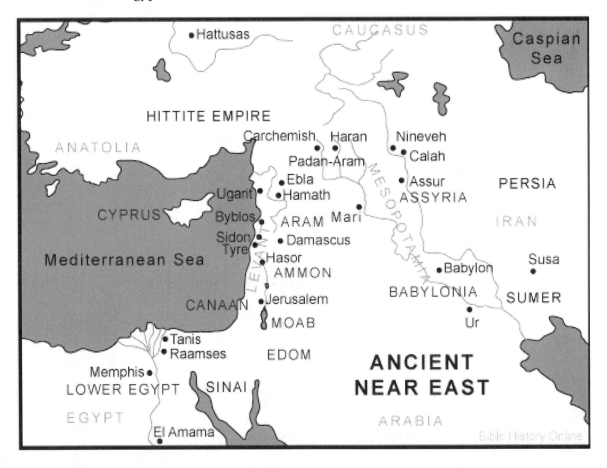

THEME: *The Pentateuch*
Lesson 4: *Genesis: Joseph—God planned it for good*

Part One: The Invitation

A. Review the unit theme.
    1. Unit theme:

    2. Lead your students in reciting the names of the five books of the Pentateuch.

    3. Lead your students in reciting the main events of Genesis, with hand motions:

Creation	Abraham
Fall	Isaac
Flood	Jacob
Tower of Babel	Joseph
Nations scatter	To Egypt

B. From last week's lesson, remind your students that Isaac was Abraham's son. Explain that Isaac had two sons, Esau and Jacob. Esau's descendants became the nation of Edom, which was south of the Dead Sea. Jacob had 12 sons, whose descendants are known as the 12 tribes of Israel or the nation of Israel. One of those sons was Joseph. He was Jacob's favorite son, and we will study about him today.

C. Introduce today's lesson topic and explain how Joseph had a destiny in God that could not be shaken.

D. Share with your students what you feel about God having a destiny for Joseph that could not be shaken.

    1. The fact that Joseph's destiny could not be changed by his brothers or employers excites me because . . .

    2. If God had a destiny for Joseph, like He did for Abraham, Isaac, and Jacob, then I can believe that He has a destiny for me and for you. This excites me because . . .

    3. If God protected Joseph's destiny, then He can protect mine and yours too. When I think about that, I feel . . .

E. Invite your students to meet with God and His destiny for them through the life and destiny of Joseph.

Part Two: The Impartation

I. Things to consider as you prepare:

A. Through the story of Joseph, what jumped out at you concerning what God wants you to share with your students?

1. You might trace the theme of reversal—Joseph seems to advance, only to fall back again, until the final promotion.

2. You might demonstrate how Joseph matures, starting with an immature response to the prophetic dreams, working through the reversals, then mature dealings with his brothers.

3. You might focus on destiny and how God evaluates our response to the circumstances of our life to see how prepared we are to fulfill our destiny.

4. You might focus on how God worked all things together for good in each situation in which Joseph found himself.

B. There are various methods of presentation.

1. You might use storytelling: telling the story in a dramatic tone of voice, using gestures.

   a. You might focus on the main points of Joseph's story, weaving it into one story, then bring out teaching points.

   b. You might use several of the stories. As you tell the stories, go one by one, and after each story, bring out a main teaching point or two related to the theme you choose.

2. You might use drama. Break into small groups and give each a story. Give the groups 10 minutes or so to prepare the story (younger groups led by an assistant teacher), then have each group present their story, in chronological order. Here are possible stories. You don't have to use all the stories—pick the ones that support your teaching points

   1. Joseph sharing the dreams.
   2. The brothers selling Joseph.
   3. Joseph at Potiphar's house.
   4. Joseph in the jail, interpreting the dreams of the baker & wine-bearer.
   5. Joseph interpreting Pharaoh's dream & giving administrative advice.
   6. Joseph meeting with his brothers.

3. You might use a mix of the two, where you tell the story, but you have students act it out in front of the others as you tell the story and direct them into their places.

II. Preparing the Impartation Segment:

      1.   The method I will use:

      2. The story/stories I will use:

The Impartation
As you introduce Joseph, put his picture up on the time line, around 1870 B.C.

On the map, point out the cities of Joseph's life—born in Padan-Aram, lived in Hebron, taken as a slave to Egypt where he spent the rest of his life.

    A. First story

      1. Telling the story:

      2. Truths to which I will draw my students' attention:

B. Second story

    1. Telling the story:

    2. Truths to which I will draw my students' attention:

C. Third story

    1. Telling the story:

    2. Truths to which I will draw my students' attention.

(If you will use more stories, use additional pieces of paper to write your notes.)

Part Three: The Application

Ask the students to write answers to the following questions in their journals.

1. How would you feel if you had dreams like Joseph that told you that you would be important some day? What do you think you would do or say?

2. How do you respond when other people mistreat you or tell lies about you?

3. Do you think that you have a particular destiny in God? What do you think it is?

Depending on which story/stories you used in your lesson, select a few questions from the questions you answered in the Biblical Foundation section.

Additional questions:

Part Four: The Impact

A. Explain to your students that God has a special destiny for each one of us. Throughout our lives, He will give us promises of how He plans to use us. These promises of destiny are really invitations. They are invitations for us to respond rightly in each situation. When we realize that we have responded wrongly, we should repent and make the changes that God tells us to make. None of us is perfect, and none of us chooses perfectly 100 percent of the time.

What is most important is that we have a "yes" in our heart to God. Joseph wanted to do the will of God, whatever it was. He trusted God to take care of him in every situation, whether as a slave, a prisoner, or as the top assistant to the Pharaoh. Joseph allowed God to defend him and to promote him; he did not try to do it himself. Yet in every situation, he did his best and he worked his hardest. In this way he not only gained the trust of those for whom he worked, but he also demonstrated that his heart was trustworthy before God. In other words, he was faithful in small things, so God increased his responsibilities.

How many of you want to walk in the full destiny that God has for you? No one can keep you from it, except yourself. No one can cheat you out of what God has for you. No one can lie about you and keep you from your destiny in God. When God wants to promote you, He can move you from the prison to the throne room in less than an hour! Only you can keep yourself from all that God has for you, if you choose to rebel against Him, if you keep choosing to respond wrongly to the situations of your life. Remember, God looks at your heart. Is there a "yes" in your heart to Him?

Invite the children to join you in prayer.

Father, thank You that You have a destiny for me, and it is good. Thank You that all that You do in my life is good. I believe that whatever happens to me, even if it doesn't seem good, You will make it bring something good to my life if I trust You. And I trust You. I say to You, "Father, I trust You. Jesus, I trust You. You are the best leader of all time, and I trust You."

Today I say "yes" to You, to all that You have for me, to all that You want me to do. Please give me grace day by day, all of my days, to say "yes" to You. Help me to respond rightly in all situations. Help me to forgive others and not to hold offenses. Help me to trust You in every circumstance. Help me to respond with wisdom and humility. Father, thank You for the plans which You have for me. I want to fulfill them all and serve You in my generation, so that You would be glorified through the name of Jesus. Amen.

B. Close by encouraging your students to share with their family what they have learned today.
1. Encourage students to share their thoughts on destiny with their families.
2. Encourage students to tell their families the stories they learned today about Joseph.
3. Encourage them to have their parents help them practice saying the five books of the Pentateuch and reciting the main events of Genesis with the hand motions.
4. Remind them about the at-home study pages at Forerunner Kids Club and encourage them to take a few minutes each day to work on them.
5. Give out the Car Talk pages.

Questions to jump-start conversation with your 7- to 12-year-old on the way home from church:

1. Who was the main person in today's lesson? [Joseph]

2. What was God's destiny for Joseph?

3. What did God speak to you today about your destiny?

4. Tell me about how Joseph responded to difficulties in his life.

This week's memory verse:
"You intended to harm me, but God intended it for good to accomplish what is now being done: the saving of many lives." (Gen. 50:20)

Key thoughts to remember:
1. From the start, God planned to use Joseph to save his entire family during the famine.
2. Joseph's destiny in God was to be a leader and in authority above his brothers. No matter what they did to him, they could not change his destiny in God.
3. Even though Joseph's circumstances changed drastically during various periods of his life, they did not change his destiny.
4. What was most important to Joseph's destiny was his correct response in every season of his life.

THEME: *The Pentateuch*

Lesson 4: *Joseph: God planned it for good*

Day One: Genesis 37:1-11

I. Read Genesis chapter 37, verses 1-11. As you do, answer the following:

    A. How old is Joseph at the start of the chapter?

    B. What does he tell his father about his brothers?

    C. How does his father (Jacob, also known as Israel) feel about Joseph?

    D. What did his father have made for Joseph? How did his brothers feel about that?

    E. What was Joseph's first dream?

    F. What happened when he told his brothers about the dream?

    G. What was Joseph's second dream?

    H. How did his father feel about that dream?

II.   Think about these things and write down your thoughts.

    A. Do you think Joseph reported his brothers' bad behavior to his father because he was jealous of them or because he felt that he was his father's representative and had a responsibility to his dad?

    B. Do you ever "tell" on your brothers or sisters or on other people? Why do you do it?

    C. Verse 11 says that Joseph's brothers were jealous of him because of the dreams, but his father kept thinking about those dreams. In other words, Jacob had a feeling those dreams were from God and was wondering what it could mean. How do you think Joseph's brothers treated him after this? How do you think his father treated him?

    D. Do you ever get any dreams that seem to be from God? Do you share them with your parents?

THEME: *The Pentateuch*

Lesson 4: *Joseph: God planned it for good*

Day Two: Genesis 37:12-36

I. Read Genesis chapter 37:12-36. As you do, answer the following:

    A. Where do Joseph's brothers take the sheep to graze? Can you find it on your map?

    B. Why does his father send him to see them?

    C. Where had they gone?

    D. What do they think when they see him coming?

    E. What does Reuben think about this? What does he convince them to do? What is his secret plan?

    F. Who comes along when Reuben is gone? What is Judah's idea?

    G. So what do the brothers do with Joseph?

    H. What happens when Reuben returns? What do they do with Joseph's special robe?

    I. What do they tell their father when they go home? How does Jacob feel?

    J. What happens to Joseph when he gets to Egypt?

II. Think about these things and write down your thoughts.

    A. How would you feel if your brothers took your special jacket from you, threw you in a pit, and later sold you as a slave?

    B. In verses 3 and 12, when Jacob interacts directly with Joseph, God inspires Moses to use Jacob's covenant-promise name, "Israel." Then when the brothers tell their lie to their father to deceive him, God inspires Moses to use his given name, "Jacob," which means "deceiver." What do you think the use of each name means to our understanding of the story?

At-Home Daily Activity Sheet 3

THEME: *The Pentateuch*

Lesson 4: *Joseph: God planned it for good*

Day Three: Genesis 39

I. Read Genesis chapter 39. As you do, answer the following:

    A. To whom was Joseph sold?

    B. How well did he do in his job? Why?

    C. To what position does he get promoted?

    D. What happened to Potiphar's household with Joseph in charge?

    E. By this point Joseph is maybe 20 to 25 years old. How does Moses describe Joseph's looks?

    F. What does Potiphar's wife think about Joseph?

    G. She invites Joseph to have an intimate relationship with her. What is Joseph's response?

    H. When Joseph refuses her again and again, what does she do to him?

    I. Does Potiphar believe her false report?

    J. What does he do with Joseph?

    K. What does God do for Joseph when he is put in prison?

    L. What job is Joseph given there?

II.   Think about these things and write down your thoughts.

    A. First Joseph becomes a slave, and then a few years later, he is falsely accused and becomes a prisoner in jail. How do you think Joseph felt about this turn of events in his life? How do you think he felt about his relationship with God?

    B. In both situations, at Potiphar's and in the jail, God blesses Joseph's work so that he was promoted? How do you think Joseph felt about this? How do you think he felt about his relationship with God?

THEME: *The Pentateuch*
Lesson 4: *Joseph: God planned it for good*

Day Four: Genesis 41

I. Read Genesis 41. As you do, answer the following:

   A. In chapter 40, after Joseph had already been in jail for a year or more, the king's baker and cupbearer were imprisoned. They each had a dream that Joseph interpreted accurately. When the cupbearer was restored to his job, he forgot to tell the king (Pharaoh) about Joseph and how he had been imprisoned unjustly. As we start chapter 41, how long has it been since the cupbearer left the jail?

   B. What are Pharaoh's dreams?

   C. Can any of Pharaoh's advisors interpret it?

   D. What does the cupbearer say?

   E. What interpretation does Joseph give?

   F. What advice does he give Pharaoh based on the dream?

   G. What does Pharaoh think about Joseph?

   H. To what position does he promote Joseph?

   I. How old is Joseph now? He was sold as a slave when he was 17. So how long has he been in Egypt already?

   J. What does Joseph do during the years of plenty?

   K. What happened when the famine hit?

II.   Think about these things and write down your thoughts.

   A. How do you think Joseph felt when the cupbearer forgot all about him? Do you think he felt that he would be in jail all his life? How would you feel?

   B. How do you think Joseph felt when suddenly he left the prison and in a few hours had become second in command to Pharaoh? Do you think he was proud of himself, or do you think he knew that promotion comes from the Lord in the Lord's time?

THEME: *The Pentateuch*
Lesson 4: *Joseph: God planned it for good*

Day Five:

I. We will skip around a bit. Read the verses indicated and answer the following:

1. Genesis 42:1-5: When Jacob's family has no food because of the famine, what do they do? Who goes?

2. Genesis 42:6-9: Does Joseph recognize the brothers? Do they recognize him?

3. Genesis 42:14-20: What test does Joseph give them?

4. Genesis 42:21-22: Why do the brothers think this is happening to them?

5. Genesis 42:24: Whom does Joseph keep with him in Egypt?

6. Genesis 43:13-15: Who goes to Egypt the second time?

7. Genesis 45:1-14:

    a. How do the brothers feel when they find out the Egyptian leader is really their brother?

    b. Why do you think they are afraid?

    c. What reason does Joseph give for what happened to him?

II.   Think about these things and write down your thoughts.

    1. Joseph endured many years of hard work and difficulties because his brothers were jealous of him and sold him into slavery. Yet he tells them in Gen. 45:5, "Don't be angry with yourselves for selling me here." Wouldn't you think that Joseph would be the angry one, not the brothers? How do you think Joseph came to such a forgiving and peaceful conclusion about the difficulties of his life?

    2. In Genesis 50:20, Joseph says to his brothers, "You intended to harm me, but God meant it for good so that many lives would be saved." Are there any situations in your life where God is working a good result from a difficult or painful situation? How can you develop a forgiving heart like Joseph and always trust in God's leadership, no matter how difficult your circumstances may be?

First Quarter, Year One: Biblical Foundations for Children
Lesson Five:
Intro to the Pentateuch: Exodus

Lesson objective: To introduce the student to the book of Exodus.

Scope of lessons on Exodus—five lessons consisting of:
1. Intro to the book of Exodus
2. The deliverance of Israel
3. The provision of God
4. The giving of the Law
5. The construction of the Tabernacle

Biblical Foundation: Background information on the book of Exodus

I. Meaning of the name and authorship:
    a. Name in English: Ex-odus. From the Greek. Means "a way out of" and refers to God making *a way out of* Egypt and out of slavery for His people, the Jews.
    b. Author: Moses. He wrote it during the years that Israel wandered in the desert.

II. Date of the Exodus: 1446 B.C. (adapted from David Malick's article on Exodus[1]):
    a. This date emphasizes the literal interpretation of the biblical numbers in Exodus 12:40, "Now the time that the sons of Israel lived in Egypt was four hundred and thirty years"; Judges 11:26, "While Israel lived in Heshbon and its villages, and in Aroer and its villages, and in all the cities that are on the banks of the Arnon, three hundred years, why did you not recover them within that time?"; 1 Kings 6:1, "Now it came about in the four hundred and eightieth year after the sons of Israel came out of the land of Egypt, in the fourth year of Solomon's reign over Israel, in the month of Ziv which is the second month, that he began to build the house of the Lord."

    b. The journey between Egypt and the Wilderness of Sinai and Mount Sinai took three months to the day (Ex. 19:1-2).

    c. It is possible that Moses composed the book during or shortly after the encampment of the people at Sinai (1446).

    d. The book occurred sometime before Moses' birth in 1526 (Ex 2).

    e. Therefore, the book of Exodus covers events around the birth of Moses to events at Mount Sinai (c. 1526-1446 BC).

---

[1] David Malick, "An Introduction to the Book of Exodus," Bible.org, http://bible.org/article/introduction-book-exodus

f.   Hill and Walton offer the following arguments for an early date:[2]

1. 1 Kings 6:1 indicates the exodus of the Israelites occurred 480 years prior to the fourth year of Solomon's reign. His fourth year is variously dated at 966/960/957 B.C., placing the exodus at 1446/1440/1437.

2. According to Judges 11:26, Israel had occupied Canaan for 300 years before the judgeship of Jephthah, which is dated between 1100 and 1050. This dates Joshua's conquest between 1400 and 1350. Adding Israel's 40 years in the desert puts the Exodus between 1440 and 1390.

3. Moses lived in exile in Midian 40 years (Acts 7:3; cf. Exodus 2:23) while the pharaoh of the oppression was still alive. The only pharaohs who ruled 40 years or more were Thutmose III (1504-1450) and Rameses II (1290-1224).

4. The Merneptah Stela (ca. 1220) indicates Israel was already an established nation at the time.

5. The Amarna tablets (ca. 1400) speak of a period of chaos caused by the "Habiru," very likely the Hebrews.

6. The early date allows for the length of time assigned to the period of the judges (at least 250 years). The late date allows only 180 years.

7. The Dream Stela of Thutmose IV indicates he was not the legal heir to the throne (i.e., the legal heir would have died in the tenth plague).

8. Archaeological evidence from Jericho, Hazor, etc., supports a 15th-century date for the Exodus.

9. Exodus 12:40 dates the entrance of Jacob into Egypt during the reign of Sesostris/Senusert III (1878-43) rather than during the Hyksos period (1674-1567).

g.   Therefore a plausible (and approximate) reconstruction would be as follows:[3]

966 = 4th full year (actually into the fifth) of Solomon's reign (971-931) when work on the Temple was begun

+44 yrs = start of David's reign (1010)

---

[2] Andrew E. Hill and John H. Walton, *A Survey of the Old Testament* (Grand Rapids, MI: Zondervan, 1991), as quoted in Malick.
[3] From this point onward, quoting Malick's "An Introduction."

+40 yrs = start of Saul's reign (1050)

+40 yrs = the time from Saul to Jephthah's statement (1050-1090)

+300 yrs = the time in the land (Jephthah's statement) (1390)

+16 yrs = Joshua's leadership (1406)

+40 yrs = wilderness wandering (1446)

This matches 1 Kings 6:1 where 966 + 480 = 1446 B.C.

III. The Pharaoh of the Exodus: Amenhotep II (c. 1436-1410)

A. It is probable that Hatshepsut (1490-1469) was the princess who reared Moses.

B. Thutmose III (c. 1490-1436?) ruled as co-regent with his stepmother until her death for 56 years. This allows for the time when Moses was in exile in Midian (cf. Acts 7:3; Exodus 2:23).

C. Amenhotep II (c. 1436-1410) may have been the Pharaoh of the Exodus. Note that the Bible does not say that he drowned but that he led a battle to the water's edge.

D. The dream inscription of Tutmose IV (c. 1410-1402?) may indicate that he was not originally intended to be Pharaoh. Therefore, his brother would have died in the plagues

IV. Route of the Exodus

A. Two Basic Views:

1. The Northern View: The Exodus took place at a lagoon bordering the Mediterranean Sea.

2. The Southern (Central) View: The Exodus took place south of Succoth near Lake Balah or Lake Timsah.

B. Textual Clues (Ex. 13:17-22; 14:1-2; Num. 33:1-49)

1. The Lord did not lead Israel by the way of the land of the Philistines (probably the Way of the Sea which was the direct route along the Mediterranean coast to Palestine) (Ex.13:17).

2. The Lord led the people by the way of the wilderness to the Red Sea (Ex.13:18).

3. The Lord led Israel from Rameses to Succoth (Ex 12:37; Num. 33:5)

4. Israel set out from Succoth and camped in Etham on the edge of the wilderness (Ex. 13:20).

5. Israel turned back and camped before Pihahiroth, between Midgol and the sea, in front of Baal-zephron, opposite it by the sea (Ex. 14:2).

6. Israel went by the Way of the Wilderness (Ex. 13:18) after crossing the Sea of Reeds and entered the Wilderness of Shur (Ex 15:22; Num 33:8) in the Northwest Sinai Peninsula.

C. Although a definitive conclusion is not possible because of the uncertainty of many of the locations in the biblical text, it seems that the Southern (Central) view matches what is known more than the northern view.

D. The Location of Mount Sinai Seems to Be Southern:

1. Some have located Mount Sinai in northwest Arabia partly on the grounds that it was considered that a volcano was required to explain the events in Exodus 19:16-25, but this is better understood as a typical Theophany. Also, Moses was not only related to the Midianites (Ex 3:1; 18:1) whose homeland was considered to be in the region of Arabia, but he was related to the Kenites who were a nomadic Midianite clan whose presence in the Sinai region is well documented (cf. Judges 1:16; 4:11).

2. The biblical text indicates that Mount Sinai was an eleven-day journey from Kadesh-barnea (Dt 1:2).

3. Elijah took 40 days and 40 nights (a long journey?) to reach Sinai from Beersheba (1 Kgs 19:8).

4. Jebel Musa (Arabic for "Mountain of Moses), or Mount Horeb, in the southern Sinai peninsula has been identified as the Mount Sinai of Moses' revelation by Christian tradition dating to the fourth century AD.[7]

V. Purposes for the Book of Exodus

A. To record for Israel her birth as a national unit and her relationship with God according to the Mosaic Covenant.

B. To narrate the battle between God and Egypt on behalf of His people to bring about their deliverance from slavery.

C. To explain the readiness of the people to accept God's revelations of the Law.

D. To describe the impatience of the people awaiting God's enthronement among the people according to His design.

E. To present the new constitution under which Israel will relate to God (the Mosaic Covenant).

F. To connect the people under God's promise to Abraham to the beginning of the theocratic kingdom under Moses.

G. To reveal God as YHWH—the one who will keep His promises.

H. To express the importance of maintaining covenant relationship with God.[4]

VI.   Major events
    a. Before the exodus of the Jews: introduction to Moses
    b. The Passover and the Exodus
    c. Mt. Sinai and the Mosaic Covenant (and Ten Commandments)

VII. Outline:

I.   Israel's problem and Moses' early life
II.   The call of Moses and journey back to Egypt
III.   Moses confronts Pharaoh
    a. Ten Plagues
        1. Water turned to blood
        2. Frogs
        3. Gnats
        4. Flies
        5. Plague on livestock
        6. Boils
        7. Hail
        8. Locusts
        9. Darkness
        10. Death of the firstborn
    b. Passover

IV.   Israel exits Egypt and God parts the Red Sea
V.   The journey to Mt. Sinai
VI.   God gives the Law
VII.   The tabernacle is built

---

[4] End Malick adaptation.

THEME: *The Pentateuch*

Lesson 5: *Introduction to Exodus*

Part One: The Invitation

A. Review the unit theme and introduce the lesson for today.

B. Ask the students to share what they can remember about the exodus of Israel from Egypt.

C. Review the names of the first five books of the Bible and the main events of Genesis.

D. Invite your students to join you on the journey of hearing from God through the book of Exodus.

Part Two: The Impartation

I. Introduce the second book of the Pentateuch: Exodus

A. Ask your students to turn to Exodus 1. Read chapter 1:7-14.

1. Explain the name of the book in English.

2. Ask the students why they think Israel needed a way out of Egypt.

3. Talk about the author of the book and when he wrote it.

4. Ask your students why they think Moses wrote this book. Explain the purpose of the book.

5. Share the outline of the book. As you go over each point, attach the appropriate picture to the time line.

I.   Israel's problem and Moses' early life
II.   The call of Moses and journey back to Egypt
III.   Moses confronts Pharaoh
      a. Ten Plagues
           1.   Water turned to blood
           2.   Frogs
           3.   Gnats
           4.   Flies
           5.   Plague on livestock
           6.   Boils
           7.   Hail
           8.   Locusts
           9.   Darkness
           10. Death of the firstborn
      b. Passover

IV.   Israel exits Egypt and God parts the Red Sea
V.   The journey to Mt. Sinai
VI.   God gives the Law
VII.   The tabernacle is built

After this, go back over the basic events of Exodus and teach the motions for the following events (hand and arm motions are given in the appendix):
Moses
"Let my people go!"
"No!"
Ten Plagues
Passover
Red Sea
Mt. Sinai
Ten Commandments
Tabernacle

Have students stand and practice the motions while saying the events (in order). Give plenty of time for students to learn it well.

B. Using the timeline, explain the timing of the exodus:

   1.   How we know the year, working backwards from Solomon:

2. Who probably was the Pharaoh's daughter?

3. Who was probably the Pharaoh of the exodus?

4. Using the map, show the possible routes of the exodus and most likely location of the Red Sea crossing.

5. Show the probable location of Mt. Sinai.

Part Three: The Application

A. Ask the students to write answers to the following questions in their journals.

1. How do you think it felt to be a slave in Egypt, working in the hot sun making bricks and building buildings day after day?

2. The Israelites had been slaves for several hundred years. The promise given to their great-great-great-great-grandfather Abraham that they would be delivered from Egypt had been passed down from generation to generation just by word of mouth, fathers telling their children. If you had been one of those slaves, would you believe deliverance was coming, or would you think it was just a nice story that would never happen. How would you feel?

3. There are countries in the world today where Christians are persecuted, imprisoned, beaten, treated as slaves. They are awaiting God's deliverance and the return of Jesus. Do you think it would be hard to have faith in a situation like that? How would you feel?

B. Break your class out into groups of two or three. Give each group a country from the following list of nations that persecute Christians. Ask the groups to pray for Christians in the country they were given, that God would give those believers steadfast faith in Him, that He would provide for them, that He would reveal Himself to them more and more, and that they would know His Presence with them. Have the students pray that the kingdom of God would come and His will would be done in each nation.

1. North Korea	11. Bhutan
2. Saudi Arabia	12. China
3. Iran	13. Pakistan
4. Afghanistan	14. Turkmenistan
5. Somalia	15. Comoros Islands
6. Maldives	16. Iraq
7. Yemen	17. Qatar
8. Laos	18. Mauritania
9. Eritrea	19. Algeria
10. Uzbekistan	20. Chechnya

Part Four: The Impact

A. Explain to your students that God delights to deliver His children. Sometimes He allows them to spend time in a difficult situation, like Joseph in the prison. Sometimes He allows them to be oppressed by political leaders or circumstances, like the Israelites. But He also delivers at just the right time. In fact, He delights in setting His children free! Lead them in the following prayer:

Father, I believe that You love me so very much. I know that You showed me your great love by sending Jesus to die in my place. Sometimes the enemy whispers to me that You don't love me because if You did, then I wouldn't have the problems I have. But I know that You show me your love and faithfulness by delivering me through my problems, not from my problems. So I say that I trust You. I trust You to deliver me at just the right time. I choose not to be offended by the circumstances You allow in my life. I believe that You do what is right and just and best.

Father, help me as I journey through my life to continue to trust You. I don't want to get offended or lose faith, even when deliverance seems a long way off. Help me to grow in faith. Your Word says that suffering produces perseverance, perseverance produces character, character produces hope, and that hope in You will not disappoint me because You pour Your love into my heart by the Holy Spirit. Fill me, Father, with faith, hope, and love in the Holy Spirit. In Jesus' name, Amen.

B. Close by encouraging your students to share with their family what they have learned today.
   1. Suggest that they share the events of the book of Exodus with their family this afternoon. Encourage them to have their parents help them practice reciting the main events of Genesis AND Exodus with the hand motions.
   2. Hand out the take-home study pages and encourage them to take a few minutes each day to work on them or encourage your students to download the at-home study pages from Forerunner Kids Club.

Questions to jump-start conversation with your 7- to 12-year-old on the way home from church:

1. What does the word *Exodus* mean?

2. Why is that the name for the second book of the Bible? What happened in that book?

3. What do you remember the most about today's lesson?

4. What did you pray about in class today?

THEME: *The Pentateuch*

Lesson 5: *Introduction to Exodus*
Day One: Exodus 1

I. Read Exodus chapter 1. As you do, answer the following:

1. In verse 5, how many of Jacob's family is in Egypt?

2. After Joseph and his brothers died, did their families leave Egypt?

3. What happened when a king came into power who didn't know anything about Joseph and how he had saved Egypt? What did that king think about all the Israelites? What did he do?

4. When the Israelites were worked hard as slaves, did their numbers decrease?

5. What did the Pharaoh command the midwives to do?

6. How do you think Moses knew the names of the midwives?

7. Did the midwives obey the king? Why?

8. In verse 20, what was God's response to the midwives?

9. In verse 22, what was Pharaoh's response?

II.   Think about these things and write down your thoughts.

1. How do you think the Israelites felt when the Egyptians enslaved them? Do you think they felt that God had abandoned them?

2. Pharaoh himself was the government in Egypt. God usually wants us to obey our government, but when the midwives disobeyed Pharaoh's command to kill the boy babies, God blessed the midwives. Why do you think this is?

3. Based on this passage, how can we know when to obey the government and when not to obey the government?

THEME: *The Pentateuch*

Lesson 5: *Introduction to Exodus*
Day Two: Exodus 2:1-15

I. Read Exodus 2:1-15. As you do, answer the following:

1. According to verse 1, from what tribe is Moses?

2. How long did Moses' mother hide him?

3. What did she do with him when she couldn't keep his presence a secret any longer?

4. Who watched over him?

5. Who found him?

6. How did his mother get him back?

7. What happened when Moses was older, probably about 3 years old?

8. Where did he grow up?

9. In verse 11, after Moses had grown up, what did he do?

10. What did he see an Egyptian do?

11. What did he do?

12. Did Pharaoh find out? What did he want to do to Moses? What did Moses do?

II.   Think about these things and write down your thoughts.

1. How would you feel if when you were three or four years old, and you had to leave your family to live with the king who had made your people slaves?

2. Do you think Moses' mother taught him about his family history and about God? Do you think Moses remembered this when he was growing up in Pharaoh's house?

3. Do you think that Moses thought of himself as an Egyptian or as an Israelite?

THEME: *The Pentateuch*

Lesson 5: *Introduction to Exodus*
Day Three: Exodus 2:15-25

I. Read Exodus 2:15-25. As you do, answer the following:

1. To where did Moses flee?

2. How did he meet the daughters of Reuel, the priest of Midian?

3. What did he do for them?

4. What did their father tell them to do?

5. When Moses decides to stay with Reuel's family, who does he marry?

6. What does he name his first son? Why does he give his son that name? (Hint: the name means "an alien there.")

7. While Moses lives in Midian, what happens to Pharaoh?

8. What do the Israelites do about their slavery?

9. When God heard their prayers, what did He remember?

10. How did God feel about the Israelites' condition?

II. Think about these things and write down your thoughts.

1. After Moses married Zipporah, do you think he planned to return to Egypt, or do you think he planned to stay in Midian for the rest of his life? He was an Israelite, who had been raised as an Egyptian, now married to a Midianite and living in Midian. Do you think he still identified with the Israelites and their God or not? Why?

2. Why did God think about His covenant with Abraham, Isaac, and Jacob? How did that covenant define His relationship with the Israelites?

THEME: *The Pentateuch*

Lesson 5: *Introduction to Exodus*
Day Four: Exodus 3:1-12

I. Read Exodus 3:1-12. As you do, answer the following:

1. At the beginning of the chapter, what is Moses doing?

2. What is the other name of his father-in-law, Reuel? (One name is his first name; one name is his family name.)

3. Where does he take the flock to feed?

4. What does he see?

5. Who calls to Moses from the bush?

6. Why does God tell him to take off his sandals?

7. How does God identify Himself?

8. What is Moses' response?

9. What does God tell Moses about His people? What has God heard and what will He do?

10. What job is God giving Moses?

11. What is Moses' response?

II. Think about these things and write down your thoughts.

1. What would you think if you saw a large bush on fire, but not burning up? How would you feel if a voice spoke to you from the bush, and the voice knew your name?

2. Moses left Egypt because Pharaoh wanted to kill him. How do you think Moses felt about having to go back to Egypt?

3. Moses had tried to help his people by killing one of the Egyptians who were enslaving them. However, that didn't work out too well for him. How do you think he felt about being sent back to deliver his people?

THEME: *The Pentateuch*

Lesson 5: *Introduction to Exodus*
Day Five: Exodus 3:13 through 4:17

I. Read Exodus 3:13 through 4:17 and answer the following:

1. Moses asks for the name of God to prove to the Israelites that their God had sent him. What name does God give to him in verse 14?

2. How does God identify Himself in verse 15?

3. With whom is Moses supposed to meet when he first returns to Egypt?

4. What are they to say to Pharaoh?

5. What does God predict will be Pharaoh's response?

6. What does God plan to do in order to change Pharaoh's mind?

7. At the start of chapter 4, Moses is not convinced this will work. What does God do with Moses' staff to convince him?

8. What does God do to Moses' hand?

9. God tells Moses to show these two signs to the elders of the Israelites. If they still don't believe that God sent Moses to deliver them, what else should he do?

10. In verse 10, what does Moses complain?

II.   Think about these things and write down your thoughts.

1. Suppose you are Moses. You were raised with people who worshipped Egyptian gods and goddesses. Now you've been living for many years with a Midianite priest who worships several other gods and goddesses. Now a voice speaks to you from a burning bush and says He is God. Why do you think Moses asked for His name? Do you think that it meant anything to Moses when God identifies Himself as the God of Abraham, Isaac, and Jacob?

2. How would you feel if a god about whom you knew very little called you to return to a nation that wanted you dead so that you could free people who are genetically your relatives, but you didn't grow up identifying with them ethnically? Would you want to obey?

First Quarter, Year One: Biblical Foundations for Children
Lesson Six:
Exodus: God Delivers His People

Objective: To demonstrate how God keeps His covenant with His people.

Key verse for this lesson: "God heard their groaning and he remembered his covenant with Abraham, with Isaac, and with Jacob. So God looked on the Israelites and was concerned about them." (Ex. 2:24-25)

Key thoughts to consider and to pass on:

1. God knew exactly when He would deliver the Israelites; He had already told Abraham how long Abraham's descendants would live in Egypt and be oppressed.
2. Moses' destiny in God was to lead God's chosen people out of Egypt. All that happened to him was intended to preserve and prepare him to do this.
3. God's people may be oppressed and enslaved, and they may feel that their prayers and groans are not being heard, but God hears and He remembers His covenant relationship with His people.
4. God's timing may not be our timing, but His deliverance is always on time for what He wants to accomplish in us.

Review from last week:

I. Israel's problem and Moses' early life
II. The call of Moses and journey back to Egypt
III. Moses confronts Pharaoh
    a. Ten plagues
        1. Water turned to blood
        2. Frogs
        3. Gnats
        4. Flies
        5. Plague on livestock
        6. Boils
        7. Hail
        8. Locusts
        9. Darkness
        10. Death of the firstborn
    b. Passover

IV. Israel exits Egypt and God parts the Red Sea
V. The journey to Mt. Sinai
VI. God gives the Law
VII. The tabernacle is built

Biblical Foundation

I. Journaling through Exodus 1-15. We're going to skip some chapters in our journaling, but you can read the entire passage from ch. 1-15, if you'd like. Because this is an extended passage, you should work on two to three Bible chapters a day so that you have ample time to pray and reflect over the Word.

1. Exodus 1:1-6: how does Moses tie this book in with the previous book?

2. How does Moses then introduce the problem?

3. Did oppressing the Israelites cause them to grow weaker?

4. What did Pharaoh instruct the midwives to do?

5. How did they respond to Pharaoh's command? Why? Would you call this a "civil disobedience?"

6. Because the midwives were not killing the baby boys at birth, what did Pharaoh command his own people concerning the baby boys?

7. From what tribe was Moses?

8. What did Moses' mother do with him? Who found him?

(Can you see the irony in this? Pharaoh commands that the baby boys be thrown into the Nile, which made them a sacrifice to Hapi, the god of the Nile, who was their god of life. Especially around the time of the flooding of the Nile, the ancient Egyptians would cast offerings, sacrifices, and amulets into the Nile to insure a good flood season—not too much water, not too little. So Moses' mother casts him into the Nile, in a sense obeying the Pharaoh, but she puts him in a basket, and he is preserved by the daughter of Pharaoh herself.)

Historical note: Very likely this princess was Hatshepsut, the daughter of Thutmose I, grand-daughter of Ahmose I, and sister of Amenmose (who died in battle). Both Thutmose I and the pharaoh preceding him (Amenhotep I) did extensive building at Thebes, the capital of Egypt at that time. Therefore there would be camps of Hebrew slaves in Thebes at that time, and the family of Moses must have been one of them.

9. Who raised Moses until he was about 3 years old? What do you think they taught him about God?

10. When he grew up, do you think he knew he was really a Hebrew? What did he do when he saw an Egyptian beating a Hebrew slave?

11. What was Pharaoh's reaction?

12. What did Moses do? Where did he go?

13. Whom did he help?

14. Whom did he marry?

15. Moses was in the desert of Midian for about forty years. What was happening with the Israelites in Egypt during this time?

16. What did the Israelites do about their condition?

17. How did God feel about their situation?

18. What did God remember? What was it about the Israelites that God was moved to act on their behalf?

19. In Chapter 3, how does God get Moses' attention?

20. How does God identify Himself to Moses? How do you think Moses knew those names? Do you think he remembered from when he was three, some seventy-five years before? Do you think he had contact with his parents when he was an adult, before he left Egypt? Do you think his father-in-law, the priest of Midian, taught him? After all, Midian was a son of Abraham by his second wife, Keturah. Do you think Jethro, as a descendant of Abraham and Midian, worshipped the one true God?

21. In verses 7-10, how does God describe His feelings for His people?

22. What is God's plan?

23. What does Moses think about this?

24. In verse 13, Moses asks for the name of God, other than "the God of your fathers." Why do you think he does this? All the Egyptian deities had names—the god Ra, the god Hathor, etc. But this God called himself "the God of Abraham, Isaac, and Jacob." This was not really a name, more like a designation.

25. What is God's response to him in verse 14?

26. What is God's comment about the identifying of Himself as "the God of Abraham, Isaac, and Jacob"?

So God says that this is His name forever, the name by which He is to be remembered from generation to generation. God identifies Himself by relationship. He doesn't say, "I am the God who created everything," even though He could have. God chooses to identify Himself with a man, with His family.

27. Verses 16-22: what is God's plan to deliver Israel?

28. Exodus 4:21-23: what does God predict will happen when Moses asks Pharaoh to let God's people go?

29. What relationship does God say that Israel has to Him?

30. What does God predict will be the final punishment inflicted upon Pharaoh that will cause him to let the Israelites leave Egypt? How do we see the Father-heart of God expressed in this?

31. Exodus 4:24-26: why do you think Moses had neglected to circumcise Gershom? Why do you think God required Gershom's circumcision before Moses fulfilled God's mission for Him? Compare Genesis 17:11 and Joshua 5:2-9.

32. Read ch. 5. How does Moses' first attempt work out?

    a. What is Pharaoh's response?

    b. What action does he take?

    c. What is the response of the Israelite foremen?

    d. What is Moses' response to God?

    e. In your relationship with God, do you feel like you can talk like that to God? After all, Moses' tone is pretty accusatory.

33. Read ch. 6. What is God's response to Moses?

34. Look at verse 2-8. See how many references God makes to family members and to relationship, to covenant.

35. What is God's purpose in delivering the Israelites, as He expressed it in verse 6-8? What will be the result?

36. What happened when Moses relayed this to the Israelites?

37. Moses lists more genealogical data in verses 14-27. He is stressing the importance of family and family relationships.

38. Read ch. 7. Look at verse 5. Why does God plan to show Egypt signs, wonders, and judgment?

39. Do you think that God was giving Egypt an opportunity to turn to Him, to leave their gods to recognize Him as the one true God and worship Him only?

40. What was the first plague/sign?

41. Look through ch. 8. What are the next three plagues? What was Pharaoh's response to each?

42. Look through ch. 9. What are the next three plagues? How does Pharaoh respond? How does God care for His people through this?

43. Read ch. 10:1-7. What does God threaten to do next? How do Pharaoh's officials respond?

44. Look at verse 8-11. God had told Moses to propose that they leave to go three days' journey into the wilderness to celebrate a festival to God, and then the plan was for the Israelites never to return to Egypt. Do you think Pharaoh is calling their bluff here? Or is God setting Pharaoh up so that Pharaoh will want all of Israel to leave forever?

45. What are the next two plagues?

46. What is Pharaoh's last compromise offer after the darkness?

47. What is Moses' response?

48. And Pharaoh's?

49. What is God's final set-up in chapter 11?

50. How do the Egyptians feel about Moses and Israel at this point?

51. How does Moses speak to Pharaoh in verses 4-8? With what emotion?

52. Read Exodus 12:1-28. Describe what the Israelites were to do. This is called the Feast of Unleavened Bread, or the Passover.

Notice that the Passover event was family-oriented. First, the lamb's blood needed to be on the doorposts of every home. Imagine if you were a firstborn and how you might have felt that night. Second, the meal was eaten by families. And if a family was too small to eat a whole lamb, then they were to share with their nearest neighboring family. Isn't it interesting that the Lord told them to determine how many people to one lamb based on how much each person would eat (verse 4). The reason for that is given in verse 10: none should be left over or kept until morning. Not a meal to plan for leftovers! So there was a deep fellowship aspect to this Passover meal.

53. What happened in the middle of the night? What was Pharaoh's response? So what did the Israelites do the very next morning?

Note: The Pharaoh of the Exodus was most likely either Thutmose III or Amenhotep II. Both had their firstborn sons die suddenly during their reigns.

54. Read Exodus 13:1-16. Because God spared the firstborn of Israel, what does He command concerning them?

Notice that the way that each firstborn is consecrated to God. God tells them the firstborn of man or animal belongs to *Him*. Firstborn animals were to be sacrificed to Him, with the exception of the donkey—it could be redeemed by the sacrifice of a lamb in its place. As for children, fathers were to redeem them back to themselves by offering a lamb for each firstborn son.

55. Look at verse 17-18. How God knows the hearts of His people! How often do you think He looks at each of us in the lessons we need to learn, and decides to take us the long way so that we don't change our mind and back off from our commitment to Him?

56. What happens to the bones of Joseph?

Think about this. Joseph spent only 17 years as a child in Canaan, then spent his entire adult life in Egypt. Yet he wanted his bones to be buried in Canaan, with his father Jacob, grandfather, Isaac, and great-grandfather Abraham, who served the God he served, the God of Abraham, Isaac, and Jacob. Having been separated from family so early in life, he wanted to be united with them in burial.

57. How did the Lord guide the Israelites as they began their journey out of Egypt?

58. In chapter 14, the Israelites end up pinned between the sea in front of them and Pharaoh's pursuing army behind them. Was Moses a poor navigator? Was this an accident?

59. Why would God intentionally put His people in such a dangerous position?

60. How did the Israelites react when they realized there appeared to be no escape for them?

61. When Moses announced that the Lord would fight for them and that they need only stand still, what do you think the people thought? Do you think they had faith that God could and would deliver them?

62. In verse 15, God says to Moses, "Why are you crying out to Me? Tell the Israelites to move on!" So

what do you think Moses first thought the Lord was going to do?

You see, having seen the Lord put the firstborn to death, Moses thought that God would fight the Egyptians while the Israelites watched. He didn't realize that God would part the waters of the sea.

63. What kind of faith do you think it took for Moses to stretch out his staff over the waters as God had commanded? Or, with the pillar of fire having taken up rear guard for them, do you think the faith of Moses was buoyed up at this point?

64. Notice the last verse in the chapter. Although throughout chapter 14, God said He was doing this so that the Egyptians would know that He is God, indeed God's acts had the same effect upon the Israelites. These adults and children had grown up as slaves. They had heard stories about their ancestors and their ancestors' God. But they had never experienced Him. Now they have experienced Him through the ten plagues, their deliverance from Egypt, and their deliverance through the Red Sea.

Archaeological note: Findings on the sea bed of the eastern upper arm of the Red Sea seem to suggest that Israel crossed here. Strange coral formations have been found in the shape of chariot wheels. You can check this out at www.arkdiscovery.com/red_sea_crossing.htm. Another site that describes more about the location of the Red Sea crossing is www.biblebelievers.org.au/bb971126.htm.

65. Read Exodus 15:1-18. How did God's acts lead them to feel about God?

66. How did God's actions lead them to feel about their future conquest of the Promised Land?

II. Look back over Exodus 1-15

A. Write a short summary of the life of Moses from birth to the time when he returned to Egypt with his wife and son.

B. Write a short summary of the deliverance of the Israelites from Egypt. Include an overview of the ten plagues.

C. Write a short summary of the deliverance of the Israelites at the Red Sea.

III. Reflect upon the following:

A. Through this study, what has God spoken to you concerning:

1. His emotions:

2. His feelings and desires concerning a family of His own, particularly relating to the deliverance of His people Israel:

3. His eternal purposes:

4. His determination to keep His promises and prophecies:

B. Finish these sentences:

1. The thought of Pharaoh ordering all the baby boys to be killed made me think . . .

2. The benefit to Moses' mother raising him until he was three was that . . .

3. When Moses killed the Egyptian, I thought that . . .

4. When I think that God would use a murderer to deliver His people, I feel . . .

5. Every time I read that God actually hardened Pharaoh's heart, I thought . . .

6. What surprised me the most about the ten plagues was . . .

7. When God set His people up for disaster, then delivered them from certain death, I learned . . .

IV. Map Time

Although for many years most Bible scholars believe the route of the Exodus placed the parting of the Red Sea at the top of the west branch of the Red Sea, with Mt. Sinai on the Sinai peninsula, recent scholarship and archeological finds have redefined the route of the Exodus and the locations of the Red Sea crossing and Mt. Sinai. The following maps reflect this new evidence:

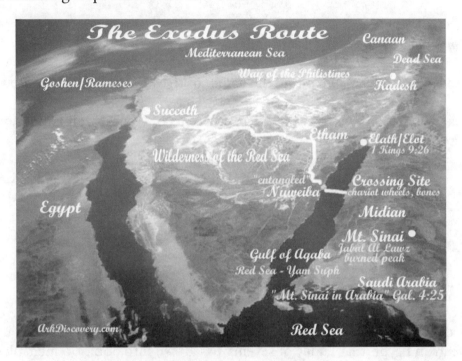

Lesson Presentation outline template

THEME: *The Pentateuch*
Lesson 6: *Exodus: God delivers His people*

Part One: The Invitation

A. Review the unit theme.
   1. Unit theme:

   2. Lead your students in reciting the names of the 5 books of the Pentateuch.

   3. Lead your students in reciting the main events of Genesis and Exodus, with hand motions:

Creation	Abraham	Moses	Red Sea
Fall	Isaac	"Let my people go!"	Mt. Sinai
Flood	Jacob	"No!"	10 Commandments
Tower of Babel	Joseph	Ten Plagues	Tabernacle
Nations scatter	To Egypt	Passover	

B. From last week's lesson, remind your students that at the start of Exodus, the children of Abraham, called the Israelites, are still living in Egypt. By now they have grown into a large nation. After 430 years in Egypt, that family of seventy has grown into 600,000 men, plus women and children. That's about three million people. But they are no longer free. Pharaoh has enslaved them because he is afraid they will challenge the Egyptians for control of Egypt.

C. Introduce today's lesson topic and explain that God had a purpose in having Jacob's family grow into a nation while they were in Egypt.
   1. The Canaanite nations continued to sin while the Hebrews were in Egypt, and when their sins reached judgment level, God brought the Israelites to conquer them as judgment.
   2. Because the Israelites knew the promise that had been given to their ancestor, Abraham, concerning the land of Canaan, they did not assimilate into Egypt as they might have done if they had been living in Canaan.
   3. God knew exactly how long they would be in Egypt and exactly when He would deliver them. He told this in advance to Abraham.

D. Share the key verse for this lesson with your students: "God heard their groaning and he remembered his covenant with Abraham, with Isaac, and with Jacob. So God looked on the Israelites and was concerned about them" (Ex. 2:24-25).

   1. Talk about the family covenant that God had with Israel then and still has now.

2. Talk about God's concern for His people.

3. Tell your students how it makes you feel to know that God honors and keeps His covenants.

E. Invite your students to meet with God and His concern for them through the deliverance of His people, the Israelites.

Part Two: The Impartation

I. Things to consider as you prepare:
   A. Through the story of Moses and the Exodus, what jumped out at you concerning what God wants you to share with your students?
      1. You might focus on the points where God intervenes: having baby Moses found by the daughter of Pharaoh; the burning bush; the ten plagues; the Passover; the parting of the Red Sea.
      2. You might focus on how God makes the impossible become possible through these same events.

   B. There are various methods of presentation.
      1. You might use storytelling: telling the story in a dramatic tone of voice, using gestures.
         a. You might focus on the main points of Moses' story, weaving it into one story, then bring out teaching points.
         b. You might use several of the stories. As you tell the stories, go one by one, and after each story, bring out a main teaching point or two related to the theme you choose.

      2. You might use drama. Break into small groups and give each a story. Give the groups 10 minutes or so to prepare the story (younger groups led by an assistant teacher), then have each group present their story, in chronological order. Here are possible stories. You don't

have to use all the stories—pick the ones that support your teaching points.
1. Miriam and Pharaoh's daughter, finding Moses.
2. Moses at the burning bush
3. Moses and Aaron confront Pharaoh; the 10 Plagues
4. A Jewish family at the first Passover
5. The parting of the Red Sea

3. You might use a mix of the two, where you tell the story, but you have students act it out in front of the others as you tell the story and direct them into their places.

II. Preparing the Impartation Segment:

As you introduce the story of Moses and the Exodus, put the picture of the woman taking the baby Moses from the water on the time line around the year 1480 B.C. The picture of the parting of the Red Sea goes around 1440 B.C.

Using the map, remind the students that the Israelites were in Egypt at this time. Show them the route of the Exodus and the location of the Red Sea crossing.

1.   The method I will use:

2. The story/stories I will use:

The Impartation

A. First story

1. Telling the story:

2. Truths to which I will draw my students' attention:

B. Second story

   1. Telling the story:

   2. Truths to which I will draw my students' attention:

C. Third story

    1. Telling the story:

    2. Truths to which I will draw my students' attention.

(If you will use more stories, use additional pieces of paper to write your notes.)

Part Three: The Application

Ask the students to write answers to the following questions in their journals.

1. Suppose you were an Israelite who had to work day after day in the hot sun, making bricks as a slave for Pharaoh. Your father had done the same, and you have been praying your whole life for God to deliver you and your people. How would you feel about God at this point?

2. When Pharaoh kept refusing Moses' requests and making the Israelites work harder, and the Israelites were angry at Moses, how do you think he felt? How do you think he felt about God?

3. When the Israelites were on the far side of the Red Sea, and they watched the waters cover up all the soldiers who had been chasing them, how do you think they felt about God then?

4. When you are in a situation that seems impossible for you, how do you feel about God? How do you feel when He helps you? How do you feel when you are still waiting for Him to help you?

Depending on which story/stories you used in your lesson, select a few questions from the questions you answered in the Biblical Foundation section.

Additional questions:

Part Four: The Impact

A. Explain to your students that God hears the groaning of our hearts and He is concerned for us. But He also has a purpose for us in each of our difficult times. God used the time of slavery to make the Israelite men and women physically strong so that they were ready for the journey across the desert. He also used it to make them desire to leave Egypt. Suppose they had never been slaves. Suppose they had only lived in an area of Egypt where the pastureland for their sheep and goats was wonderful, and they had plenty of food from their gardens. And then Moses had come to tell them that God wanted them to leave their homes and walk across the desert to a land where they would have to fight the inhabitants so that they could claim it for their own. Do you think they would have wanted to do that? Probably not. So God let the Egyptians enslave them for about 100 years or more, and then they remembered that God had promised their ancestor, Abraham, a land for them. Then they cried out for God to fulfill His promises for them. Then they cried out for deliverance. And when God sent a deliverer, they were ready to leave.

Sometimes God allows us to go through difficult times in order to prepare our hearts for what He has for us. Sometimes we feel that He has left us alone, that He has forgotten us or forgotten His promises to us. So we cry out to God, and God says, "Good! Now you are talking to me! Come closer! Talk to me more." God hears our cries, and He is concerned for us. He has good plans for us, and we can trust Him that at just the right time, He will break through and deliver us. He is never late; He is always on time.

Have your students think about how God displayed His great power on behalf of the Israelites. Not only did He disrupt the natural state of things for the Egyptians through the ten plagues, but He also protected the Israelites from those disasters again and again. God showed Himself mighty on their behalf. All the power that God has at His disposal He will use to help you in your situations in life. You can trust Him.

Invite the children to join you in prayer.

Father, thank You that You have made us a part of Your family. Thank You that we are Your children and You care for us. You have a plan for us, to make us stronger through the problems in our life. You strengthen our faith. You help us to grow in our love for You. You draw us nearer to You. We are grateful and we say that we trust You.

At this point, ask if there are any children who are experiencing difficulty in their life right now or whose family is going through a difficult time. Ask these children to stand or to raise their hand. Have the children around them turn to them, lay hands on them, and pray for them. Have your assistant teachers circulate among the groups, helping to pray.

Guide the groups by encouraging them to ask the child for whom they will pray what is the need—what is the prayer request. Give them a few moments to do that. Then encourage the children to begin praying. Also encourage them to listen to the Lord and see if He has any words for them to give as encouragement to the person for whom they are praying.

When it seems that most of the groups have finished, close this time in prayer.

B. End the class by encouraging your students to share with their family what they have learned today.
   1. Encourage students to share their thoughts on God's intervention with their families.
   2. Encourage students to tell their families the stories they learned today about Moses.
   3. Encourage them to have their parents help them practice saying the five books of the Pentateuch and reciting the main events of Genesis and Exodus with hand motions.
   4. Remind them about the at-home study pages at Forerunner Kids Club and encourage them to take a few minutes each day to work on them.

CAR TALK

Questions to jump-start conversation with your 7- to 12-year-old on the way home from church:

1. Tell me how God delivered His people from Egypt.

2. Tell me about the picture of Jesus that we can see in Passover.

3. How do you think you would have felt if you had been trapped between the Red Sea and Pharaoh's army? Would you have been worried?

4. Why do you think God let His people be slaves for so long before He delivered them from Egypt?

Memory verse for this week:

"God heard their groaning and he remembered his covenant with Abraham, with Isaac, and with Jacob. So God looked on the Israelites and was concerned about them." (Ex. 2:24-25)

Key thoughts to remember:

1. God knew exactly when He would deliver the Israelites; He had already told Abraham how long Abraham's descendants would live in Egypt and be oppressed.
2. Moses' destiny in God was to lead God's chosen people out of Egypt. All that happened to him was intended to preserve and prepare him to do this.
3. God's people may be oppressed and enslaved, and they may feel that their prayers and groans are not being heard, but God hears and He remembers His covenant relationship with His people.
4. God's timing may not be our timing, but His deliverance is always on time for what He wants to accomplish in us.

THEME: *The Pentateuch*

Lesson 6: *Exodus: God delivers His people*
Day One: Exodus 4 & 5

I. Read Exodus 4:29 through 5:23. As you do, answer the following:

A. With whom did Moses and Aaron meet first?

B. What was the response of the elders?

C. To whom did they go next?

D. What did they tell him?

E. What was Pharaoh's response to them?

F. What did Pharaoh tell the slave drivers to do?

G. How did the Israelites respond to this? What did they say to Moses and Aaron?

H. How did Moses feel about this? What did he say to the Lord about it?

II.   Think about these things and write down your thoughts.

1. God told Moses that He would deliver his people out of Egypt, yet He told Moses to ask for only a three-day vacation for the Israelite slaves to offer sacrifices to God. How do you think Moses felt about this?

2. Suppose you were an Israelite foreman, and you were told that not only did your people now have to gather their own straw for the bricks, but they had to produce the same number of bricks as when the straw was provided for them. Then, when your people don't make enough bricks, the Egyptian slave drivers beat you. How would you feel? Would it be hard for you to trust that God would really deliver you?

THEME: *The Pentateuch*

Lesson 6: *Exodus: God delivers His people*
Day Two: Exodus 6

I. Read Exodus 6. As you do, answer the following:

    A. According to God in verse 1, why will Pharaoh let the Israelites go?

    B. In verse 3, God is saying, "Abraham, Isaac, and Jacob knew me as the God who provides for their needs, yet didn't they also know me as the One who ever Is?" In light of God being the One who always is, and who never changes, what does God remind Moses about in verse 4?

    C. Because of that covenant, what did God hear in verse 5?

    D. What does God tell Moses to declare to the Israelites?

        a. In verse 6, what will the Lord do for them?

        b. In verse 7, how will the Lord relate to them?

        c. In verse 8, to where will He bring them?

    E. When Moses related all this to the Israelites, how did they feel about it? Why?

    F. What does God tell Moses to do next?

    G. What is Moses' evaluation of himself and his ability to lead?

    H. Verses 14-27 are an interlude, an aside, to identify Moses and Aaron for us. Here Moses records who were the leaders of the tribes of Jacob's three oldest sons at this time. In particular, he tells us about his own tribe, the tribe of Levi. Remember that the word used for "son of" also means "descendant of." When we add together the years of Levi's life with the years of Kohath's life and the years of Amram's life, we come up with the number of years that the Israelites lived in Egypt. So Moses is giving us the names of the three major generations leading up to his own birth. Amram is his father, but Kohath is something like his great-grandfather.

II.   Think about these things and write down your thoughts.

    A. Why do you think that God is so concerned about them understanding His Name? How does who God is relate to His covenant with His people?

    B. How important is the reputation of God's name to you?

THEME: *The Pentateuch*

Lesson 6: *Exodus: God delivers His people*
Day Three: Exodus 7:1 through 8:15

I. Read Exodus 7:1 through 8:15. As you do, answer the following:

   A. In verses 1-5, what does God predict will happen?

   B. What was the first miracle they performed for Pharaoh?

   C. Who mimicked it?

   D. What did Aaron's staff do to their staffs?

   E. How did Pharaoh respond?

   F. What was the second miracle?

   G. Could Pharaoh's magicians imitate it?

   H. How did Pharaoh respond? What did he do?

   I. What did the Egyptians have to do?

   J. Seven days after the water turned to blood, what was the second plague that God sent against Egypt?

   K. What was Pharaoh's response? What did he promise?

   L. Did he keep his promise?

II.   Think about these things and write down your thoughts.

   A. Suppose you were Moses, and God told you to give a prophetic word to a world leader who would reject you. How would you feel?

   B. How do you think the Egyptians felt about Moses and the Israelites when their water turned to blood? What do you think they thought Pharaoh should do about it?

THEME: *The Pentateuch*

Lesson 6: *Exodus: God delivers His people*
Day Four: Exodus 8:16 through 9:35

I. Read Exodus 8:16 through 9:35. As you do, answer the following:

    A. What was the third plague?

    B. Could the magicians imitate it?

    C. What was their conclusion?

    D. What was Pharaoh's response?

    E. What was the fourth plague?

    F. Did the plague affect the area of Egypt where the Israelites lived?

    G. What was Pharaoh's response? What did he propose to Moses?

    H. When the flies left, how did Pharaoh respond?

    I. What was the fifth plague?

    J. Did the plague affect the area of Egypt where the Israelites lived?

    K. What was Pharaoh's response?

    L. What was the sixth plague?

    M. What was Pharaoh's response?

    N. What is God's message to Pharaoh before the next plague? Pharaoh was treated like a god by the Egyptians. How do you think he felt to be challenged by a God he could not see?

    O. What was the seventh plague?

    P. Did Pharaoh's officials believe Moses? What happened?

    Q. How did Pharaoh respond?

THEME: *The Pentateuch*

Lesson 6: *Exodus: God delivers His people*
Day Five: Exodus 10:1 through 11:10, and 12:29-36

I. Read Exodus 10:1 through 11:10, and 12:29-36 and answer the following:

    A. What is the eighth plague?

    B. What do Pharaoh's officials tell him before the plague begins?

    C. When Moses tells Pharaoh that he wants everyone, even the women and children, to go into the wilderness to worship God for three days, what does Pharaoh suspect?

    D. What do the locusts eat?

    E. What is the ninth plague? How long does it last? Does it affect the Israelites?

    F. What deal does Pharaoh try to make with Moses? Does God accept this offer?

    G. Read Exodus 11:1-10 and 12:29-26 to find out about the final plague. What is it?

    H. Even the son of Pharaoh died. What did Pharaoh do next?

    I. How did the Egyptians feel about the Israelites leaving?

    J. What did they give the Israelites?

II.   Think about these things and write down your thoughts.

    A. Suppose you are an Egyptian. For several weeks now, you have been experiencing strange weather conditions and attacks of insects and animals. You've heard that it has been caused by the Israelites' God, and your gods seem unable to do anything about it. How do you think you would feel about your gods and Israel's God?

    B. Suppose you are an Israelite. You've heard about the God of your forefathers, but you've been a slave all your life, and He has never helped you before this. Now you've seen all that He inflicted on Egypt just to free you and your people. How do you think you feel about Him?

First Quarter, Year One: Biblical Foundations for Children
Lesson Seven:
Exodus: God Provides for His People

Objective: To demonstrate how God provides for His family.

Key verse for this lesson: Exodus 16:12, "I have heard the grumbling of the Israelites. Tell them, 'At twilight you will eat meat, and in the morning you will be filled with bread. Then you will know that I am the Lord your God.' "

Key thoughts to consider and to pass on:
1. God knows what we need and He will provide for all our needs, even our physical ones.
2. Often God provides exactly what we need, no more and no less. We must learn contentment with what He gives.
3. Complaining is not a good solution. Better to pray for what we need, rather than complain about our circumstances.
4. Trust God to intervene, even when it looks impossible.

Review From Last Week:

I. Israel's problem and Moses' early life
II. The call of Moses and journey back to Egypt
III. Moses confronts Pharaoh
    a. Ten Plagues
        1. Water turned to blood
        2. Frogs
        3. Gnats
        4. Flies
        5. Plague on livestock
        6. Boils
        7. Hail
        8. Locusts
        9. Darkness
        10. Death of the firstborn
    b. Passover
IV. Israel exits Egypt and God parts the Red Sea
V. The journey to Mt. Sinai
VI. God gives the Law
VII. The tabernacle is built

Biblical Foundation

I. Journaling through Exodus 15-17. We'll start at Exodus 15:22.

1. Exodus 15:22. For three days they travel through the desert without finding what? After the third day, they find water, but what is the problem with it?

2. What is the response of the people?

3. What is the response of Moses?

4. What is the response of God?

5. What conditional promise did the Lord make with Israel at this time?

6. To where did they travel next? What did they find there?

Note: Palm trees don't mean much to us, but to them, seventy palm trees meant coconut water to drink and coconut meat to eat. It meant coconut husks to burn so that they could have cook fires. Also, the fact that there were twelve springs and seventy palm trees means it was a very large oasis.

7. At the start of chapter 16, the Israelites have been traveling together for about five weeks. They are running out of the food they brought along with them. Read verse 3 to see how they remembered their time in Egypt. What did they think they remembered?

8. Verse 4: what is God's response to their problem?

9. What instructions does God give concerning the collection of this food He will provide?

10. In verses 6-8, why does Moses say that the Lord will provide them with food?

11. Who appears to the people as a cloud of glory in verse 10? Why do you think He did this?

12. What did God provide for them to eat that night?

13. What did they find on the ground in the morning?

Notice that they were asking each other, "What is it?" *Manna* means *what is it?*

14. How much did Moses instruct them to gather?

15. What do you think Moses was referring to when he said that "when they measured it out, he who gathered much did not have too much, and he who gathered little did not have too little. Each had what he needed." Was he pointing to each one's ability to measure by eye what his or her family

needed? Or was he speaking about God's ability to provide for us exactly what we need? That it doesn't depend on us putting in a lot of effort or a small amount of effort, but that God sees us respond to what He gives, and He makes it to be exactly what we need.

16. What happened when some of the families worried that there wouldn't be any for the next day so they kept some overnight?

17. So then it came to Thursday night, and Moses instructed them, "Tomorrow is the day before the Sabbath. So gather twice as much manna tomorrow morning. Cook it, bake it, prepare it on Friday, and keep half overnight Friday night to eat on the Sabbath." Verse 27 says that some people went out on the Sabbath morning to gather manna, but there wasn't any there. Why do you think they went out?

Probably for the same reason that some people had first tried to keep some overnight—they were worried about providing for themselves. They feared that if they kept some overnight, it would spoil, so they tried their own plan. They figured that if it had been there every morning for six mornings, then it was a natural occurrence and would be there on morning seven. They didn't believe the supernatural aspect of God's provision for them, nor did they understand the need to do everything exactly as God had commanded them.

18. Read verses 31-36. Notice that this is a short explanation about manna. It's not a part of the chronological story. It is a parenthetical section. In it, Moses names the food and describes it. He rehearses his instructions concerning it. He tells us about how he instructed Aaron to gather a sample of manna for future generations to see, and where to put it—before the Testimony. Now at this point, God had not yet given them "the Testimony." In Exodus 25:16, God tells Moses that when God gives the Testimony, he is to put it in the ark of the covenant. Moses tells us here that God provided the manna for forty years until they came to enter the promised land. Therefore, we can assume that it was some time after the construction of the ark of the covenant and the giving of the Testimony that Moses gave this instruction to Aaron. Moses also explains the measure that the Israelites used to measure the manna.

19. Read Exodus 17:1-7. What happened when they arrived at Rephidim?

20. How did the people respond?

21. So God is now providing daily food for them and has already made the bitter water sweet, not to mention having parted the Red Sea. Do they trust Him yet?

22. What does God tell Moses to do?

23. Why does Moses re-name the place?

Note: *Massah* means testing; *Meribah* means quarreling. So after all that God has done for them, they still do not believe the Lord is with them.

24. Read Exodus 17:8-15. What is the next thing that happens to them while they are in Rephidim?

25. What happened when Moses held his staff up?

26. What happened when he let it down?

27. What did they do when he got tired and couldn't hold it up any longer?

28. Could Joshua conquer alone? Could Moses? Did it take a team effort?

29. Why do you think Moses built an altar after the battle?

30. Why did the Lord command Moses to write the account of this battle?

II. Look back over Exodus 15-17

A. Write a short summary explaining how God provided for the Israelites in the first months of their journey. Include a section on water, a section on food, and a section on protection from invaders.

B. For each of those sections, write a truth or application that you learned or observed.

   a. Provision of water

   b. Provision of food

   c. Protection in battle

III. Reflect upon the following:

A. Through this study, what has God spoken to you concerning:

   1. His emotions:

   2. His feelings and desires concerning a family of His own, particularly relating to the deliverance of His people Israel:

   3. His eternal purposes:

   4. His determination to keep His promises and prophecies:

B. Finish these sentences:

   1. If I had been a weary traveler in the desert, and was thirsty with no water in sight, I would have thought . . .

2. If I had been Moses, with all those people complaining, and nothing I could do about it, I would have . . .

3. When I read about how some people didn't follow the commands of the Lord concerning the manna, I thought . . .

4. Reading about the complaints of the Israelites and their inability to trust the Lord convicted me that . . .

5. I could see similarities between the problems of the Israelites and problems in my life such as . . .

6. What surprised me the most about God's continued provision was . . .

THEME: *The Pentateuch*
Lesson 7: *Exodus: God provides for His people*

Part One: The Invitation

A. Review: This week there is not as much biblical content to teach, so this is a good week to do a thorough review of the stories and truths taught so far.

    1. Unit theme: God is a Father who desires a family.

    2. Lead your students in reciting the names of the five books of the Pentateuch.

    3. Lead your students in reciting the main events of Genesis and Exodus, with hand motions:

Creation	Abraham	Moses	Red Sea
Fall	Isaac	"Let My people go!"	Mt. Sinai
Flood	Jacob	"No!"	10 Commandments
Tower of Babel	Joseph	Ten Plagues	Tabernacle
Nations scatter	To Egypt	Passover	

    4. Review the stories.

      a. Explain that we want to review the Bible stories we have studied so far by acting them out. Explain that when you call out a story title, you would like several students to volunteer to act it out. As you call out each title, pick student volunteers to act it out, and send them to a corner or area of the room to practice. Once all the stories have been assigned, allow five minutes for them to practice, then call the groups back. Have them act out their stories one by one.

      OR

      b. Explain that we will review the Bible stories we have studied so far by telling them. Explain that when you call out a story title, you would like a student to volunteer to tell as best as he or she can.

      c. Possible stories to review:

        i. Adam and Eve: the fall of ,an
       ii. Cain and Abel
      iii. Noah and the Ark
      iv. God's promises to Abraham
       v. Lot and the destruction of Sodom
      vi. Abraham sacrifices Isaac

    vii.   Joseph is sold by his brothers

   viii.   Joseph in jail and interprets the baker's and cupbearer's dreams

    ix.   Joseph interprets Pharaoh's dream

B. Close the review by rehearsing the story of Moses to them: Moses was found by Pharaoh's daughter after his mother hid him in a basket among the reeds along the river. He was with his family until he was about 3 or 4, and after that he was raised in the palace as the son of Pharaoh's daughter. When he was about 40, he killed an Egyptian guard who was beating a Hebrew slave, and he had to flee into the desert. He lived for forty years in the desert of Midian, and then God spoke to him out of a burning bush and sent him back to Egypt to deliver his people. Pharaoh said, "No!" so God sent ten plagues: water turned to blood; frogs; gnats; flies; plague on livestock; boils on the skin; hail; locusts; darkness; and death of the firstborn. Each time Pharoah refused to let the Israelites go until the last plague. After his own son died, Pharoah let them go. But a few days later he changed his mind and sent his army after them. God led the Israelites to the Red Sea, where they were trapped between the water in front and the soldiers in back. Then God parted the waters and they walked across on dry ground. When the soldiers followed, God waited until all the soldiers were in the water, then let the waters fall back across and drown the soldiers, delivering the Israelites.

C. Introduce today's lesson topic and explain that God provides for His people, even where it seems impossible.

D. Share the key verse for this lesson with your students: "I have heard the grumbling of the Israelites. Tell them, 'At twilight you will eat meat, and in the morning you will be filled with bread. Then you will know that I am the Lord your God'" (Ex. 16:12).

    1.   Talk about how God heard their groans in our last lesson, and He was concerned about them. The groans were due to being oppressed, and the groans were prayers addressed to God.

    2.   Talk about how God is hearing their grumbling in this lesson. The grumbling is complaining because they fear they will not have food. The grumblings were *not* prayers; they were addressed to Moses or spoken to each other. However, God still heard them and took care of them.

    3.   Talk about how sometimes we groan in prayer, and sometimes we just complain, and yet God hears us even when our attitude is not right. Talk about how it makes you feel to have a God who takes care of you so well.

E. Invite your students to meet with God and His concern for them through His provision for His people, the Israelites.

Part Two: The Impartation

Things to consider as you prepare:
A. Through the story of God's provision for His people, what jumped out at you concerning what God wants you to share with your students?

1. You might focus on the physical provision of water and food and how we can trust God to take care of us.
2. You might focus on the spiritual application of water and food (compare 1 Cor. 10:3-4); talk about God providing for us streams of living water (Jn. 4:14) and Jesus being the bread of life (Jn. 6:35).
3. You might bring out the intercession aspect of Moses praying for the solution to the water and food problems and of his intercession for the army that led to their victory.

B. There are various methods of presentation.
1. You might use storytelling: telling the story in a dramatic tone of voice, using gestures.
   a. You might focus on the main points of Moses' story, weaving it into one story, then bring out teaching points.
   b. You might use several of the stories. As you tell the stories, go one by one, and after each story, bring out a main teaching point or two related to the theme you choose.
2. You might use drama. Break into small groups and give each a story.
3. You might use a mix of the two, where you tell the story, but you have students act it out in front of the others as you tell the story and direct them into their places.

II. Preparing the Impartation Segment:

A. The method I will use:

B. The story/stories I will use:

III. The Impartation

    A. First point

        1. Telling the story:

        2. Truths to which I will draw my students' attention:

    B. Second point

        1. Telling the story:

        2. Truths to which I will draw my students' attention:

C. Third point

    1. Telling the story:

    2. Truths to which I will draw my students' attention:

Part Three: The Application

Ask the students to write answers to the following questions in their journals.

1. Suppose you were an Israelite who had been walking day after day in the hot sun. You've been walking for three day without fresh water, and you just drank the last water in your goatskin canteen. What would you be thinking? How would you feel about God at this point?

2. If you woke up in the morning, and there were strange disks scattered all over the ground, and your mother told you to gather it for breakfast because it was the food you would be eating from now on—food from God—how do you think you would feel? The Israelites ate it for forty years, three times a day. Do you think you would grow bored of eating the same thing that long?

3. How do you think you would have felt if you had seen Moses strike the rock in the name of God and water began to pour out of it? What do you think you would have said or done?

4. Is there anything you are worried about today, something that you feel you need and you wonder if God will provide it? What is it and how will you trust God about it?

Part Four: The Impact

A. Explain to your students that God knows what we need even before we need it. Moses made it clear that God was leading them step-by-step to each place where they camped. God knew that the water was not drinkable. He planned it that way so that He could show Himself mighty on their behalf when He caused the branch to turn the water drinkable. He knew that the Israelites would run out of food, and He had already planned to send the manna. He planned to sustain them in the desert for forty years because He loved them, had a plan for them, and wanted to show Himself mighty on their behalf *so that* they would love Him and worship Him.

Even so, God plans to provide for us. He plans to lead us into places where we don't yet have what we need. We can complain and worry, like the Israelites, *or* we can choose to trust God to provide. The Apostle Paul told us in 1 Corinthians 10 that what happened to the Israelites in the desert happened as an example to us so that we would not react the way that they did.

We can trust God to provide what we need. King David said that he never saw God's people forsaken by Him. When we find ourselves in need, we can pray in faith, knowing that we pray to a Father who will not give us a stone when we ask for bread. Jesus told us that when we pray in faith, God our Father will provide all that we need, everything all the way up to the gift of Himself, the Holy Spirit.

Are you lonely and needing comfort? Ask Him, and He will comfort you. Are you needing wisdom and understanding? Ask Him, for He gives wisdom to anyone who asks. Whatever you need, spiritually, emotionally, physically, ask and He will provide.

Invite the children to join you in prayer.

Father, thank You that You have made us a part of Your family. Thank You that we are Your children and You care for us. You have a plan for us, to make us stronger through the problems in our life. You strengthen our faith. You help us to grow in our love for You. You draw us nearer to You. We are grateful and we say that we trust You.

At this point, ask if there are any children who are experiencing difficulty in their life right now or whose family is going through a difficult time. Ask these children to stand, or to raise their hand. Have the children around them turn to them, lay hands on them, and pray for them. Have your assistant teachers circulate among the groups, helping to pray.

Guide the groups by encouraging them to ask the child for whom they will pray what is their need—what is their prayer request. Give them a few moments to do that. Then encourage the children to begin praying. Also encourage them to listen to the Lord and see if He has any encouraging words to give to the person for whom they are praying.

When it seems that most of the groups have finished, close this time in prayer.

B. End the class by encouraging your students to share with their family what they have learned today.

1. Encourage students to share their thoughts on God's intervention with their families.
2. Encourage students to tell their families the stories they learned today about Moses.
3. Encourage them to have their parents help them practice saying the five books of the Pentateuch and reciting the main events of Genesis and Exodus with the hand motions.
4. Remind them about the at-home study pages at Forerunner Kids Club and encourage them to take a few minutes each day to work on them.

Questions to jump-start conversation with your 7- to 12-year old on the way home from church:

1. Last week you studied about God delivering His people from Egypt. That means that this week they must have been in the desert. What did they do about water?

2. How about food? What did they eat? What was that like? How did they get it?

3. Were they ever attacked by enemies? How did God protect them?

Memory verse for this week:

"I have heard the grumbling of the Israelites. Tell them, 'At twilight you will eat meat, and in the morning you will be filled with bread. Then you will know that I am the Lord your God.'" (Ex. 16:12)

Key thoughts to remember:
1. God knows what we need and He will provide for all our needs, even our physical ones.
2. Often God provides exactly what we need, no more and no less. We must learn contentment with what He gives.
3. Complaining is not a good solution. Better to pray for what we need, rather than complain about our circumstances.
4. Trust God to intervene, even when it looks impossible.

THEME: *The Pentateuch*

Lesson 7: *Exodus: God provides for His people*
Day One: Exodus 12:1-30

I. Since we didn't study through this at home last week, we'll do it this week. Read Exodus 12:1-10, about the first Passover. As you do, answer the following:

1.   What does each man take for his household?

2.   What if his household is small?

3.   What kind of lamb should they pick? How old? Male or female? Sheep or goat?

4.   Notice in verse 3 that they pick out the lamb on the tenth day of the month. According to verse 6, they take care of the lamb for four days. What happens on the fourteenth day of the month?

5.   What do they do with the blood in verse 7?

6.   In verse 12 and 13, God explains why they put the blood there. What explanation does He give?

7.   In verses 8 and 9, how does God tell them to eat the meat from the lamb?

8.   In verse 11, how are they supposed to dress for the meal?

9.   In verse 15, what are they told to remove from their house at the start of the Passover?

10. In verses 24-28, why does God tell them to keep celebrating the Passover every year?

II.   Think about these things and write down your thoughts.

1.   Suppose you were the older son in the home. How would you feel when you heard that God was going to put to death the oldest son in every family? How would you feel about the Passover lamb?

2.   Suppose you were an Israelite child, and your family picked out a cute lamb for the Passover feast, and then you had to take special care of it for four days, feeding it and combing its wool. How do you think you would feel when it was time to sacrifice the lamb? Why do you think God wanted them to become friends with the lamb they would sacrifice?

THEME: *The Pentateuch*

Lesson 7: *Exodus: God provides for His people*
Day Two: Exodus 14

I. Since we didn't study through this at home last week, we'll do it this week. Read Exodus 14. As you do, answer the following:

1.   According to verse 1, who directed the Israelites to camp by the sea?

2.   After the Israelites had left Egypt, after the Egyptians had buried their dead sons and recovered their wits, what did Pharaoh and his officials think about having let them go?

3.   What action did Pharaoh take?

4.   How many of his best chariots did he send?

5.   Did he send soldiers on foot as well?

6.   Where do they catch up to the Israelites?

7.   What do the Israelites think?

8.   What does Moses think?

9.   How does the angel of God protect them?

10. What does God do with the sea?

11. What does God do about the Egyptian army?

12. How did the Israelites feel about that?

II.   Think about these things and write down your thoughts.

1.   The Israelites had never seen miracles. All that they had experienced of the power of God had been the plagues, which were like judgments. They had no understanding of how God could deliver. If you had never heard of God's great power, would you have been worried about the Red Sea situation?

2.   Would you be amazed if something like that happened today? What are your expectations about what God can and can't do?

THEME: *The Pentateuch*

Lesson 7: *Exodus: God provides for His people*
Day Three: Exodus 16

I. Read Exodus 16. As you do, answer the following:

1. What is the problem in verses 2 and 3?

2. What is God's solution in verse 4?

3. In verse 7, what does Moses say they will see in the morning?

4. What did God give them to eat that night?

5. What did they find in the morning after the dew evaporated?

6. How much were they supposed to gather each day?

7. What happened if they kept some overnight to eat the next day?

8. What about on the sixth day—how much were they supposed to gather? Could they keep it overnight for the Sabbath?

9. On the morning of the Sabbath, was there any on the ground? Why not?

10. Were there some people who were not paying attention to the instructions?

11. What did the people call this bread?

12. What did it taste like?

13. How did they cook it?

14. For how long did God provide it for them to eat?

II. Think about these things and write down your thoughts.

1. Moses told the people that in the morning they would see the glory of God. But in the morning, what they saw was the manna on the ground. How was that seeing the glory of God?

2. Is it surprising to you that God provided supernaturally for His people in the desert?

At-Home Daily Activity Sheet 4

THEME: *The Pentateuch*

Lesson 7: *Exodus: God provides for His people*
Day Four: Exodus 17

I. Read Exodus 17. As you do, answer the following:

1. What problem did they encounter at Rephidim?

2. How did the people respond?

3. How did Moses respond? What did he do?

4. What did God instruct Moses to do? Who was he to take with him?

5. What happened when Moses struck the rock?

6. What two names did Moses give the place? (The first name means "testing" and the second name means "quarreling.")

II. Think about these things and write down your thoughts.

1.   It seems that every time the Israelites run into a problem or setback, they complain. They didn't seem to believe that God was for them, that God would take care of them. How do you feel when you hit a difficulty in your life, or when you need something that you don't think you can get? What is your "contentment level?" What is your "faith level?"

2. Why do you think that God told Moses to take some of the elders with him when he went to hit the rock? (Hint: if he didn't take them, and he went out in front of the people, and he hit the rock, and the water came, would the people believe that God provided it, *or* would they think that Moses just found a stream?)

3. Why do you think God was concerned that they knew it was a miracle?

THEME: *The Pentateuch*

Lesson 7: *Exodus: God provides for His people*
Day Five: Exodus 18

I. Read Exodus 18 and answer the following:

1. What were the names of the sons of Moses? What did each name mean?

2. Who came to visit Moses? Whom did he bring with him?

3. When he arrived, what did Moses tell him?

4. What was Jethro's response?

5. What did Jethro offer to God?

6. What did Moses do all the next day?

7. What problem did Jethro see in what Moses was doing?

8. What did Jethro suggest?

9. Did Moses listen to his father-in-law? Did he do what Jethro suggested?

II. Think about these things and write down your thoughts.

1. After Moses told Jethro about how the Lord (Yahweh) delivered the Israelites, Jethro said, "Now I know that Yahweh is greater than all the other gods." Then he offered sacrifices to the Lord. Jethro was a priest in his hometown. Apparently he worshipped several gods. Why do you think this story brought him to have faith in the Lord? Do you think he recognized that the Lord was the *one* true God, or do you think he just saw the Lord as having more power than other deities?

2. Look at verse 21. What kind of men did Jethro suggest should become judges and officials? Do you think those are good characteristics for leaders to have? Why?

First Quarter, Year One: Biblical Foundations for Children
Lesson Eight:
Exodus: Israel Relates to God through the Law

Objective: To demonstrate how the law was given in the context of family, that it was about creating relationship and managing relationship, not about creating separation from relationship.

Key verse for this lesson: "Now if you obey me fully and keep my covenant, then out of all nations you will be my treasured possession. Although the whole earth is mine, you will be for me a kingdom of priests and a holy nation." (Ex. 19:5-6)

Key thoughts to consider and to pass on:
1. God desired a group of people to be His treasured possession, chosen from among the peoples of the world.
2. God chose the Israelites to be His people.
3. In the Old Testament, God gave the law as requirements for Israel to keep in order to be related to Him as His people.

Review from last week:

I.   Israel's problem and Moses' early life
II. The call of Moses and journey back to Egypt
III. Moses confronts Pharaoh
    a.   Ten plagues
          1.   Water turned to blood
          2.   Frogs
          3.   Gnats
          4.   Flies
          5.   Plague on livestock
          6.   Boils
          7.   Hail
          8.   Locusts
          9.   Darkness
          10.   Death of the firstborn
    b.   Passover

IV. Israel exits Egypt and God parts the Red Sea
V.   The journey to Mt. Sinai
VI. God gives the Law
VII. The tabernacle is built

Biblical Foundation

I. Journaling through Exodus 19-24.

1. Exodus 19: after traveling for three months, where do the Israelites arrive?

2. Moses ascends the mountain and calls to the Lord. What does God tell him to say to the people?

   a. How does God refer to His mighty works on Israel's behalf?

   b. What are the conditions of this covenant?

   c. What are the benefits of the covenant?

3. What is Israel's response when Moses relates this to them?

4. What instructions does God give Moses as to how the people are to prepare themselves for two days prior to God meeting with Moses?

5. On the third day, when they woke up, what was the weather like?

6. How did the Israelites feel?

7. Notice that in verse 16, a trumpet blast woke them up. Was Moses having someone sound reveille? In verse 19, we read that as they went to stand at the foot of the mountain, the sound of the trumpet grew louder and louder. So it seems that an angel was sounding the trumpet, not man, since both times Moses includes it in the description of what was happening at the mountain, particularly at the mountaintop.

8. When God calls Moses to come up the mountain, what does God reinforce as Moses arrives topside?

9. What does Moses assure Him?

10. Didn't God know this already? Why do you think God is bringing this up again with Moses?

11. Whom does God send Moses back down to get?

12. Why do you think God kept reinforcing the command that the people were not to force their way up to see Him? Do you think there were some people in the group of Israelites and foreigners who would want to see God in order to believe He existed? Or to be sure that He was going to continue to take care of them? Or who were tired of an invisible God? Or wanted to see what He looked like? Or who wanted to present themselves as an alternate leader to take over because they thought

they could do a better job than Moses? God said that if anyone so much as touched the mountain, they would die. It would seem that God really didn't want to have to kill anyone, so He kept warning them.

13. Exodus 20:3-17 lists what we call the Ten Commandments.

   a. What is the first commandment, in verse 3?

      i. Write it in your own words.

      ii. What does it mean to you?

   b. What is the second commandment, in verse 4?

      i. Write it in your own words.

      ii. What does it mean to you?

      iii. In verse 5-6, what is the reason God gives for this command?

      iv. Would you agree that God desired to show love to them rather than punish them?

   c. What is the third commandment, in verse 7?

      i. Write it in your own words.

      ii. What does it mean to you?

   d. What is the fourth commandment, in verse 8?

      i. Write it in your own words.

      ii. What does it mean to you?

      iii. In verse 9-11, what is the reason God gives for this command?

   e. What is the fifth commandment, in verse 12?

      i. Write it in your own words.

      ii. What does it mean to you?

      iii. What is the blessing associated with keeping this commandment?

    f.   What is the sixth commandment, in verse 13?

        i.   Write it in your own words.

        ii.   What does it mean to you?

    g.   What is the seventh commandment, in verse 14?

        i.   Write it in your own words.

        ii.   What does it mean to you?

    h.   What is the eighth commandment, in verse 15?

        i.   Write it in your own words.

        ii.   What does it mean to you?

    i.   What is the ninth commandment, in verse 16?

        i.   Write it in your own words.

        ii.   What does it mean to you?

Devil's advocate moment: Does this mean "don't ever lie"? Or, when it says, "Don't give false witness against your neighbor," is it talking about a legal or community situation? For example, don't say that your neighbor took your lamb when you really lost it to the wolf.

    j.   What is the tenth commandment, in verse 17?

        i.   Write it in your own words.

        ii.   What does it mean to you?

14. Verses 18-21 are parenthetical; Moses is reminding us where he is and where the people are during this time. He is reminding us of how the people were feeling about the situation.

15. In verses 22-26, God is giving some basis guidelines about how they were to worship Him.

    a.   How does God feel about making statues of spirits who desire to be worshipped?

    b.   What is the first kind of altar He describes?

    c.   What is the second kind? What are the directions for making this kind of altar? (In other words, use field stones.) Why do you think using a tool on the stones would defile it?

16. Why should the altars be low enough that they don't need steps to reach the top?

17. Read through chapters 21-23. These are regulations the Lord gave to order societal relationships and to prevent or resolve conflicts. Read through and jot down any that interest or surprise you.

18. Exodus 24: after God gives Moses this much information, He sends Moses and Aaron back to the people to read it to them and get a response. He also sends an invitation. What is that invitation and to whom is it given?

19. When Moses recited God's commands and laws to the people, what was their response?

20. What did Moses do the next morning?

21. What did he do to represent the twelve tribes?

22. What task did he give to some of the young men?

23. What did Moses do with the blood of the sacrifice?

24. Moses again read the law to the people. When they made the covenant to keep it, what did Moses do with the blood?

25. When Moses sprinkled them with the blood, what did he say to them?

26. Compare that with the words of Jesus in Luke 22:20. Based on Moses' words, what was Jesus saying to His disciples (and to us)?

27. Who went up the mountain that afternoon?

28. What did they see?

29. What is the importance of verse 11? Think in terms of our theme—that God is a Father who desires a family.

30. So at the end of this time of worship and "family picnic," God calls Moses to do what?

31. What does Moses instruct the elders to do?

Note: By "wait here," Moses is indicating that the whole Israelite camp is to stay camping at the base of the mountain. Notice he puts Aaron and Hur in charge. (For you Star Trek fans, if he were Captain Picard, he would have said, "Aaron, you have the bridge.")

32. Moses and Joshua ascend to the top of the mountain, and the cloud of the glory of the Lord descended. Moses stopped short of the cloud until what? How long did that take?

33. For how many days did Moses (and presumably Joshua) stay on the mountain?

II. Look back over Exodus 19-24

A. Write a short summary explaining the giving of the law and the making of the covenant.

B. Write out your thoughts about how the law and the giving of the law relates to the theme of God being a Father who desires a family. What do these laws have to do with family?

III. Reflect upon the following:

A. Through this study, what has God spoken to you concerning:

1. His emotions:

2. His feelings and desires concerning a family of His own, particularly regarding His relationship with His people Israel:

3. His eternal purposes:

B. Finish these sentences:

1. If I had been an Israelite standing at the foot of the mountain, I would have felt . . .

2. If I had been an elder climbing the mountain to see God, I would have felt . . .

3. If I had been Joshua, climbing up higher with Moses, I would have felt . . .

4. When I read through the relationship laws, I thought . . .

5. If I had been an Israelite, and I heard that every seventh year I had to plant nothing and leave all my fields fallow, I would have thought that . . . or worried that . . .

6. What surprised me the most about the laws was . . .

7. When I read that God was sending an angel ahead of them, to guard and lead them, and that they were to pay attention to him and listen to him, I thought . . .

Lesson Presentation outline template

THEME: *The Pentateuch*
Lesson 8: *Exodus: Israel relates to God through His law*

Part One: The Invitation

    A. Review:

        1. Unit theme: God is a Father who desires a family

        2. Lead your students in reciting the names of the five books of the Pentateuch.

        3. Lead your students in reciting the main events of Genesis and Exodus, with hand motions:

Creation	Abraham	Moses	Red Sea
Fall	Isaac	"Let my people go!"	Mt. Sinai
Flood	Jacob	"No!"	10 Commandments
Tower of Babel	Joseph	Ten Plagues	Tabernacle
Nations scatter	To Egypt	Passover	

    C. Introduce today's lesson topic and explain that God gave the Israelites laws about how to relate to Him and to each other.

    D. Share the key verse for this lesson with your students: "Now if you obey me fully and keep my covenant, then out of all nations you will be my treasured possession. Although the whole earth is mine, you will be for me a kingdom of priests and a holy nation." (Ex. 19:5-6)

        1. Remind your students that a covenant is an agreement that brings about a relationship of commitment between God and His people. Remind them that the covenant God made with Abraham was *unconditional*: God would keep it no matter what Abraham did. Explain that the covenant that God made with Israel here in Exodus is *conditional*. God said, "*If* you obey, *then* you will be My treasured possession."

            a. The Apostle Paul told us in Romans that the Israelites who didn't obey and who didn't believe were cut off from the vine that is Israel, and those of us Gentiles who have faith and believe are grafted into that vine.

            b. As Peter said in I Peter 2:9-11 when he wrote to the believers scattered through the nations, "You are a chosen people, a royal priesthood, a holy nation, a people belonging to God . . . Once you were not his people, but now you are the people of God; once you had not received mercy, but now you have received mercy."

            c. You might mention that we call the covenant God made with Abraham "The Abrahamic covenant" and the covenant that God made with the nation of Israel at the time of Moses "The Mosaic covenant."

        2. Talk about the purpose of the law. While God gave the law in order to help the Israelites get along with one another and relate to Him, God did not intend that anyone

be saved by keeping the Law.

     a. Paul says in Galatians 3:10 that if we rely on our keeping the law for our salvation, then we are cursed because if we fail to keep even one tiny part of the law, then we have failed all together. Since we all are human and fail to do anything perfectly all the time, we are cursed from the start if the law were the way to salvation.

     b. Paul also said that Jesus redeemed us from the curse of the law when He died on the cross because He became cursed on our behalf.

     c. Paul goes on to explain that the law was given to point out our imperfection and to show us our need for a Savior. The job of the law, in terms of salvation, was to lead us to Jesus.

3. Explain that God did not give us the law so that we would fail and He could punish us. God gave us the law to show us the break in relationship that happened when Adam and Eve sinned in the garden, and to show us that we, too, are sinners. He used the law to show us that we needed the relationship repaired, and then He sent Jesus to repair it. God gave the law out of His great love for us!

E. Invite your students to meet with God and His desire for relationship with them through His giving of the law to His people, the Israelites.

Part Two: The Impartation

I. Things to consider as you prepare:

    A. Through the story of the giving of the law, what jumped out at you concerning what God wants you to share with your students?

      1. You might focus on God's desire to relate to the Israelites through the law.

      2. You might focus on the purpose of the law, both for Israelites and for us.

      3. You might focus on how the various groups of people related to God throughout the process —the people, the elders, Joshua and Aaron, and Moses.

    B. There are various methods of presentation.

      1. You might use storytelling: telling the story in a dramatic tone of voice, using gestures.

        a. You might focus on the main points of the giving of the Law, telling it chronologically, then bring out teaching points,

        b. You might break it into several sections. As you tell the sections one by one, bring out a main teaching point or two related to the theme you choose.

        c. If you are talking about the purpose of the law for the Israelites and for us, you might tell the story of the giving of the law, then move into Galatians 3 for the teaching points.

      2. You might use drama. Break into small groups and give each a section.

      3. You might use a mix of the two, where you tell the story, but you have students act it out in front of the others as you tell the story and direct them into their places.

II. Preparing the Impartation Segment:

1. The method I will use:

2. The story/stories I will use:

III. The Impartation

On the timeline, add the picture of Moses and the two tablets with the Ten Commandments. Put it next to the picture of the parting of the Red Sea.

On the map, point out the location of Mt. Sinai so that the students remember where the Israelites are at this point in their history.

A. First point

    1. Telling the story:

    2. Truths to which I will draw my students' attention:

B. Second point

    1. Telling the story:

    2. Truths to which I will draw my students' attention:

C. Third point

    1. Telling the story:

    2. Truths to which I will draw my students' attention.

Part Three: The Application

Ask the students to write answers to the following questions in their journals.

1. Suppose you are an Israelite and you wake up to a trumpet blaring. You hear thunder and lightening, too. You go to your tent door, and you see a thick cloud over the mountaintop. You know that Moses has warned everyone *not* to touch the mountain or they will die. You know that Moses will meet with God on the mountaintop. How do you feel about God? What do you think about Him?

(After a few moments, you might ask if they would feel that God was very scary or very holy or very different from them, separated from them, hard to know, hard to be close to . . .)

2. God wants us to know how to treat each other nicely. Much of the law gives directions about how to resolve conflicts and get along. How do you feel knowing that God is so concerned for us to be able to get along and live in peace with each other.

3. Even though God gave us the law, He knew that we weren't perfect and that we would break the law from time to time. That's why He planned to send Jesus to take our punishment for breaking the law. We learned that God sent the law to be a school teacher to lead us to our Savior, Jesus. How do you feel when you make a mistake and do what you are not supposed to do? (Give the children a minute or two to write in their journals). Many times we feel guilty when we do wrong. Guilt is good if it leads us to repent from our sin and receive God's forgiveness and grace. Our relationship with God is based on grace, not on our ability. As we grow in the Lord and learn to keep His commands more and more, still we can only obey because of His grace working in our hearts the desire and ability to obey Him. How do you feel about God's grace for you?

4. What would you like to tell God about His law and His grace? You can write your feelings in a prayer to Him in your journal.

Part Four: The Impact

A. God wants each of us to be part of His family. We said that God gave the law so that we would see that we ourselves are sinners and would understand our need for a Savior. You know, some people think that if they were in the garden of Eden that they would *not* have eaten the forbidden fruit. So God wrote out some laws for us to keep. And none of us can keep every single one. Only Jesus could, because He was the God-man. He was fully God and fully man, and the human part of Him surrendered to the God-part of Him all the time. So He never sinned. Because He was the only perfect man, the only perfect human, He qualified to take our punishment in our place. And because He was the infinite God-man, His death paid the penalty for every one of us.

Is there anyone here this morning who has never prayed to Jesus and accepted His payment for their sins? If you have never asked Jesus to be your personal Savior, we want to invite you today to pray and ask Him. If you are trusting in your own ability to be good and keep God's laws, then you need a savior. The Apostle Paul said that if you will say with your mouth that Jesus is Lord, that He is the one and only God-man who made you and owns you, and that if you believe in your heart that He died for your sins and was raised back to life by God the Father, then you will be saved.

If you want to pray to Jesus, to tell Him that you believe He is Lord and that He died for you, stand up right where you are. Stand up, and we will pray with you.

(Give time for children to respond. Maybe you have a small group, and you know that they all have professed faith in Christ. Still give time for them to respond, because for some of the younger children, this lesson on the law may have brought them to an understanding that they never had before and some may feel that they want to pray again now that they have understanding of their guilt before God and the grace in Jesus' sacrifice.)

Invite the children to join you in prayer

Father, thank You that You sent Your only Son, Jesus, to be born as a human, like us, and to take our punishment on Him when He died on the cross. We were cursed when we broke Your law, and He took that curse upon Himself. Jesus, I believe that You are the one true God-man and that You died in my place. I deserved death, but You died so that I could live in fellowship with God. Jesus, I believe that You are Lord, that You have the right of authority and control in my life. I receive You as my Savior. Thank You that now I am part of God's family. Thank You for the grace of God which is at work in my heart. I love You, Jesus! Father God, I love You! Teach me how to fellowship with You. Talk to me every day, Jesus! I want to be Your friend. Father, be glorified in my life through the name of Jesus, Amen.

B. End the class by encouraging your students to share with their family what they have learned today.
   1. Encourage students to share their thoughts on God's law and grace with their families.
   2. Encourage students to tell their families the story of the giving of the Law.
   3. Encourage them to have their parents help them practice saying the five books of the Pentateuch and reciting the main events of Genesis and Exodus with the hand motions.
   4. Remind them about the at-home study pages at Forerunner Kids Club and encourage them to take a few minutes each day to work on them.

Questions to jump-start conversation with your 7- to 12-year-old on the way home from church:

1. I understand that God made a covenant with Abraham, and then He made another covenant with the Israelites at Mount Sinai. So what is a covenant?

2. God gave them a lot of laws at Mt. Sinai. Why did He do that?

3. What happens if we break even one little law? What did God do so that we could be restored to relationship with Him, even though we break His law?

Memory verse for this week:

"Now if you obey me fully and keep my covenant, then out of all nations you will be my treasured possession. Although the whole earth is mine, you will be for me a kingdom of priests and a holy nation." (Ex. 19:5-6)

Key thoughts to remember:
1. God desired a group of people to be His treasured possession, chosen from among the peoples of the world.
2. God chose the Israelites to be His people.
3. In the Old Testament, God gave the law as requirements for Israel to keep in order to be related to Him as His people.

THEME: *The Pentateuch*

Lesson 8: *Exodus: Israel relates to God through His law*
Day One: Exodus 19:1-13

I. Read Exodus 19:1-13. As you do, answer the following:

    A. Where are the Israelites camped now?

    B. God calls to Moses from the mountain. What does God say will happen to the Israelites if they obey Him fully and keep His covenant?

    C. God says that even though the whole earth belongs to Him, the Israelites will be uniquely His. How? What will they be?

    D. When Moses tells the elders and the people about this, what is their response to God's proposal?

    E. What does God tell Moses He will do next? (verse 9)

    F. Why will He do this?

    G. What does God tell Moses to tell the people to do in order to prepare for His presence?
        a. Consecrate themselves for how many days?

        b. What are they to wash?

        c. What needs to be placed around the bottom of the mountain?

    H. Can the people go up the mountain? Can they touch the mountain?

    I. What happens if they do?

    J. When can they go up the mountain?

II.   Think about these things and write down your thoughts.

God told Abraham that He would make Abraham's descendants into a great nation. When God promised this, there were no conditions—God would do this no matter how the Israelites acted. God promised that He would give the land of Canaan to Abraham's descendants, no matter how the Israelites acted. But now He makes a new covenant with them: *if* they obey all His commandments, *then* they will be His treasured possession, a holy nation. Why do you think they have to obey Him in order to be His treasured possession?

THEME: *The Pentateuch*

Lesson 8: *Exodus: Israel relates to God through His law*
Day Two: Exodus 19:16-25

I. Read Exodus 19:16-25. As you do, answer the following:

1. In verse 16, what happened on the third day?

2. How did everyone in the camp feel about it?

3. To where did Moses lead all the people?

4. What was happening on Mt. Sinai? What did it look like? Why?

5. For whom did God call?

6. What did God remind Moses when he reached the place where God met him?

7. Whom did God tell Moses to bring up with him?

II. Think about these things and write down your thoughts.

1. Think about what Mount Sinai looked like when God descended on it. If you had been one of the Israelites, how do you think you would have felt? What do you think your opinion of God would have been after that? How would you have felt about God?

2. Suppose you were Aaron. You see the fire, the smoke. You feel the ground shaking. You hear the thunder and the trumpet blaring louder and louder. Your brother goes up the mountain and disappears into the cloud, and then he comes back down to tell you that God wants to meet with you, too. How do you think you feel? Do you think Aaron was scared, worried, or excited? Or what?

At-Home Daily Activity Sheet 3

THEME: *The Pentateuch*

Lesson 8: *Exodus: Israel relates to God through His law*
Day Three: Exodus 20:1-17

I. Read Exodus 20:1-17. This is what we call the Ten Commandments. As you read them, write them in your own words:

A. What is the first commandment, in verse 3?

   a. Write it in your own words.

   b. What does it mean to you?

B. What is the second commandment, in verse 4?

   c. Write it in your own words.

   d. What does it mean to you?

   e. In verse 5-6, what is the reason God gives for this command?

   f. Would you agree that God desired to show love to them rather than punish them?

C. What is the third commandment, in verse 7?

   g. Write it in your own words.

   h. What does it mean to you?

D. What is the fourth commandment, in verse 8?

   i. Write it in your own words.

   j. What does it mean to you?

   k. In verse 9-11, what is the reason God gives for this command?

E. What is the fifth commandment, in verse 12?

   l. Write it in your own words.

   m. What does it mean to you?

   n. What is the blessing associated with keeping this commandment?

F. What is the sixth commandment, in verse 13?

   o. Write it in your own words.

p. What does it mean to you?

G. What is the seventh commandment, in verse 14?

q. Write it in your own words.

r. What does it mean to you?

H. What is the eighth commandment, in verse 15?

s. Write it in your own words.

t. What does it mean to you?

I. What is the ninth commandment, in verse 16?

u. Write it in your own words.

v. What does it mean to you?

J. What is the tenth commandment, in verse 17?

w. Write it in your own words.

x. What does it mean to you?

THEME: *The Pentateuch*

Lesson 8: *Exodus: Israel relates to God through His law*
Day Four: Exodus 23:20-33

I. Read Exodus 23:20-33. As you do, answer the following:

    A. Whom did God send with the people of Israel?

    B. What was this angel's job?

    C. God promised to bring them into the land of the Canaanites, Amorites, and other nations. When the Israelites got there, those people would have their own religions. How were they supposed to relate to these religions? (verse 24)

    D. If they worship the Lord their God only, what will God do for them?

    E. In verses 27-28, what was God's battle plan?
    F. Was this going to be a quick battle, a quick war to conquer the promised land?

    G. Why was God going to do this little by little? What would happen if He did it all at once?

    H. What did God promise their boundaries would one day be? (This was fulfilled when David was king.)

    I. What did God warn them in verse 32?

II.   Think about these things and write down your thoughts.
    A. God sent with them an angel, His own representative. God told them to obey what this representative told them and not to rebel against him because God's Name was in this representative. This representative was given to them to lead them, to advise them, and to bring them to the promised place. God has given you a representative like this who lives inside you—the Holy Spirit. How do you relate to the Holy Spirit? Do you take time to listen for His voice speaking to you? When you have decisions to make, do you ask God to guide you by His Spirit inside you?

    B. Pray the following:
       1. Thank You, God, that You have given me the Holy Spirit to guide me.
       2. Father, I want to hear Your voice. Tune my ears to hear Your Spirit speak to me. Help me to know when it is Your voice that I hear.
       3. I declare to You my desire to hear and obey You.

THEME: *The Pentateuch*

Lesson 8: *Exodus: Israel relates to God through His law*
Day Five: Exodus 24

I. Read Exodus 24 and answer the following:

1. Whom did the Lord invite to come up the mountain to worship Him?

2. What happened when Moses went and told the people all the Lord's words and laws?

3. What did he build early the next morning?

4. Then they make some offerings. Moses reads the book of the covenant to them—that means he reads the laws and the promises to them. When the people affirm that they will obey the Lord, what does Moses do with the blood?

5. What do Moses, Aaron, Aaron's sons, and the seventy elders do next?

6. Whom did they see?

7. What was under His feet? (John called this the sea of glass.)

II. Think about these things and write down your thoughts.

1. Maybe it sounds strange that, after the people agreed to the covenant of the law, Moses sprinkled them with blood. Hebrews 9:18-22 explains the law requires a blood sacrifice and that "without the shedding of blood there is no forgiveness of sin." The blood of bulls and goats was shed in the old covenant of the Law. Whose blood was shed in the new covenant that God made with us? Hebrews 10:22 says that we may draw near to God with a sincere heart and in confidence of faith, because our hearts have been sprinkled to cleanse us from a guilty conscience. What did God sprinkle our hearts with? Yes, the blood of Jesus! Just like Moses sprinkled the people.

2. In verse 11, we read that the leaders saw God, and they ate and drank. It doesn't mean they had a picnic with God. It's more like they saw God on His throne, and they lived to tell about it. It is also a picture of fellowshipping with Him. They worshipped Him and fellowshipped with Him. At this point in history, everyone else worshipped idols made of stone that represented spirit beings. But they had never seen these spirit beings. Only the Lord revealed Himself to man. Do you think that the elders were astonished to see this God their ancestors served? What do you think they told their family and friends when they returned to the camp?

First Quarter, Year One: Biblical Foundations for Children
Lesson Nine:
Exodus: Israel Relates to God through the Tabernacle

Objective: To introduce the student to the tabernacle of Moses and meeting God through the furniture of the tabernacle.

Key verse for this lesson: "Have them make a sanctuary for me, and I will dwell among them. Make this tabernacle and all its furnishings exactly like the pattern I will show you." (Ex. 25:8-9)

Key thoughts to consider and to pass on:
1. God desired a place where He could dwell with His people and where they could meet to worship Him.
2. God gave specific instructions for this tabernacle because it is a picture about how He relates to us.

Review from last week:
I. Israel's problem and Moses' early life
II. The call of Moses and journey back to Egypt
III. Moses confronts Pharaoh
    a. Ten plagues
        1. Water turned to blood
        2. Frogs
        3. Gnats
        4. Flies
        5. Plague on livestock
        6. Boils
        7. Hail
        8. Locusts
        9. Darkness
        10. Death of the firstborn
    b. Passover

IV. Israel exits Egypt and God parts the Red Sea
V. The journey to Mt. Sinai
VI. God gives the Law
VII. The tabernacle is built

Biblical Foundation

I. Journaling through Exodus 36-40

Note: in Exodux 25-31, God gives Moses the blueprint for the tabernacle. In Exodus 36-40, Moses gives a concise account of how they fulfilled the instructions. For the purpose of teaching our students, we will focus on the fulfillment account. However, if you are reading the entire book of Exodus, you will want to read through chapters 25-35.

1. Exodus 36:1: who was appointed to oversee the building of the tabernacle? Why?

2. How did they get the supplies for building?

3. How generous were the people?

4. What did Moses finally tell the people about their offerings?

5. What is described in verses 8-13?

6. What is described in verses 14-18?

7. What is described in verse 19?

8. What is described in verses 20-33?

9. What did they do with the acacia wood to make it beautiful and special, in verse 34?

10. What is described in verses 35-36?

11. What is described in verses 37-38?

All of the above describes the actual tabernacle itself. It was a tent-like structure covered first by goat hair curtains, then by ram skin dyed red and sewn together, and lastly by sea cow hides, sewn together, making it weatherproof.

12. What is described in Exodus 37:1-9?

13. What is described in verses 10-16?

14. What is described in verses 17-24?

15. What is described in verses 25-28?

16. What is described in verse 29?

17. What is described in Exodus 38:1-7?

18. What is described in verse 8?

19. What is described in verse 9-20?

This is the external courtyard of the tabernacle ,which measured 150 feet by 75 feet, surrounded by a fence about seven feet in height. The fence was made of linen hangings held by pillars. The entrance curtain was embroidered.

20. Read through Exodus 38:21-31 and appreciate all the expensive materials that went into making the tabernacle.

In total, this was about a ton of gold. At $400 an ounce, this is $12,800,000. At current prices, which is around $900 an ounce, this is $28,800,000.

It was 3.75 tons of silver. At $14 an ounce, this is $1,680,000.

It was 2.5 tons of bronze. At $1.40 an ounce, this is $7000.

21. Where did these former slaves get all this gold, silver, and bronze? Go back to Exodus 12:35-36.

22. In Exodus 39, we read the description of the special clothing for the high priest, and the normal clothing for all the priests (Aaron and his sons.)

    a. In verses 22-26, we read of the blue robe, which was ankle-length and opened in the front. It had embroidered pomegranates around the hem, and between each pomegranate was attached a little gold bell. According to Exodus 28:35, why did the Lord want bells on the hem?

    b. Verses 27-29 describes the linen tunic, which went under the blue robe.

    c. Now go back to verses 2-6. This describes the ephod, which was something like a vest, but not open in the front. It was connected at the shoulders, slipped over the head, and tied at the sides. At the shoulders, where front and back were joined by shoulder pieces, there was an onyx stone on each side. What was engraved on it and why? Look at Exodus 28:9-13 for a complete answer.

    d. Verses 8-21 describe the breastpiece, which attached to the front of the ephod. What precious stones were on it, what did they symbolize, and what was on each stone?

       Look back to Exodus 28:29 to see why the Lord commanded this breastpiece be worn by the high priest.

e. Verses 30-31 describe the turban which Aaron wore on his head. Look back to Exodus 28:36-38 to see why it was inscribed "Holy to the Lord."

23. Read through Exodus 40. As you do, compare the furnishings and their placement with the picture below (note: not drawn exactly to scale).

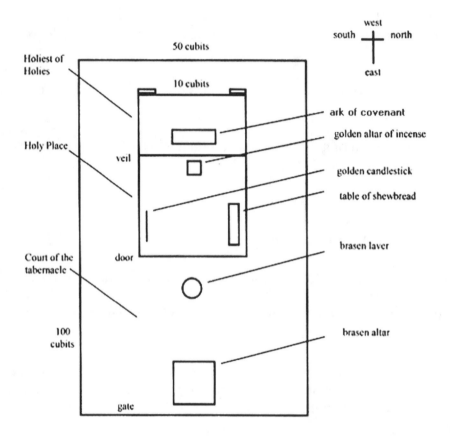

24. Once the tabernacle was completed, what happened?

25. How did God direct His people concerning their travels after the tabernacle was built?

26. Why was it so important that Moses follow God's instructions exactly for building the tabernacle? Look at Hebrews 8:5.

II. Symbolism in the tabernacle of Moses

A. **The fence and the gate:** the people of God are separate from the world, and the gate is Jesus (John 10:7)

B. **The brazen altar:** salvation through the shed blood of the Lamb.

C. **The brazen laver:** represents cleansing. Titus 3:5-6 speaks of the washing of regeneration. Ephesians 5:26 speaks of the washing of the Word which cleanses the church.

D. **The table of showbread:** Jesus said, "I am the bread of Life" (Jn. 6:35-51). Also reminds us that "man shall not live by bread alone, but by every word that comes from the mouth of God."

E. **The golden lampstand:** represents Jesus as the light of the world (Jn. 8;12; 9:5). Also represents the people of God, as in Revelation 1:20 where the seven lampstands represented seven churches.

F. **The altar of incense:** in Scripture, incense represents prayers (Rev. 5:8). Here we see the prayers of the people ascending before the presence of God.

G. **The veil** between the Holy Place and the Holy of Holies: This represented the relational separation between God and His people while only animal blood was being shed. When Jesus died on the cross, then the veil was torn, and we were given access (Hebrews 10:19: we have confidence to enter the most holy place through the blood of Jesus). Notice the progression: The people were allowed into the court of the tabernacle to bring their sacrifices and offerings. The priests could go into the holy place. But only the high priest could go into the holy of holies, and only at the appointed time.

H. **The Ark of the Covenant:** this is the place where the presence of God was manifested.

III. Reflect upon the following:
A. Some people use the furniture of the tabernacle (or the temple) as a devotional pattern.
1. Enter the gate and come to the bronze altar: "Jesus, thank You that You are the door, that You made the way for me to come before the Father. Thank You that by Your blood I can enter the holy of holies and come before the very throne of God."
2. Confession at the bronze laver: Examine your heart for sin. Repent. Rejoice in the Lord Jesus who washes you clean.
3. The light of the candlesticks: Invite the Holy Spirit to give you wisdom and revelation in the knowledge of God.
4. The table of showbread: Use this time to eat the bread of the Word; meditate upon the

Word of God.

5. The altar of incense: Bring your prayers and intercession before the Lord.
6. The ark of the covenant: Meditate upon the Lord.
7. Depart with thanksgiving in your heart!

Give this a try, if you have never used this pattern before. Afterwards, reflect upon your experience. Ask the Lord if He wants you to share this simple outline with your students or not.

B. Finish these sentences:

1. What surprised me the most about the tabernacle and its construction was . . .

2. What bothered me the most about the tabernacle was . . .

3. Thinking about the people freely giving all that gold to the work of God made me realize . . .

4. If I had been the craftsman working on the ark of the covenant, I would have felt . . .

5. When I read about the precious stones bearing the names of the tribes, I thought . . .

6. When I read that the glory of the Lord filled the tabernacle, I felt . . .

7. If I had been an Israelite, and each morning looked toward the tabernacle to see if the glory cloud had moved or not, I would have felt . . .

THEME: *The Pentateuch*
Lesson 9: *Exodus: Israel relates to God through the tabernacle*

Part One: The Invitation

A. Review:

    1. Unit theme: God is a Father who desires a family.

    2. Lead your students in reciting the names of the five books of the Pentateuch.

    3. Lead your students in reciting the main events of Genesis and Exodus, with hand
       motions:

Creation	Abraham	Moses	Red Sea
Fall	Isaac	"Let my people go!"	Mt. Sinai
Flood	Jacob	"No!"	10 Commandments
Tower of Babel	Joseph	Ten Plagues	tabernacle
Nations scatter	To Egypt	Passover	

B. Introduce today's lesson topic and explain that God gave the Israelites laws about how to relate to
    Him and to each other.

C. Share the key verse for this lesson with your students: "Have them make a sanctuary for me, and I
    will dwell among them. Make this tabernacle and all its furnishings exactly like the pattern I will
    show you." (Ex. 25:8-9)

Talk about God's desire to dwell with His people. From Genesis 3, where God walked with Adam and
Eve in the cool of the day, to Revelation 21:3, where the New Jerusalem descends to the new earth, and
God announces, "Now the dwelling of God is with men, and He will live with them. They will be His
people, and God himself will be with them and be their God."

D. Invite your students to meet with God and His desire for relationship with them through the
tabernacle of Moses.

Part Two: The Impartation

I. Things to consider as you prepare:
    A. Aspects to bring out while teaching about the tabernacle
        1. Reinforce the idea that from God's perspective, the tabernacle was a place for Him to dwell, so that He would live with His people.
            a. It was not just a place of worship and sacrifice. It was the dwelling of God on earth.
            b. Before the giving of the Holy Spirit at Pentecost, God did not dwell in man. Now we believers are living tabernacles, living temples of God, because God the Holy Spirit dwells in us.
        2. As you describe each piece of furniture in the tabernacle, describe its practical function, then give the spiritual picture.

    B. For this lesson, since it is more visual, in terms of a building/tent, with furniture, and less of a story, we suggest that you use either a large diagram of the tabernacle, or build a model.

        1. www.the-tabernacle-place.com has for sale a flannel set tabernacle and a "build-a-model" tabernacle, a tabernacle overhead transparencies set, and a tabernacle PowerPoint presentation.

        2. www.christianbook.com has a paper model (cardboard) of the tabernacle and a wall chart.

        3. www.jewishsoftware.com has a cardboard/paper model of the tabernacle for purchase.

II. The Impartation

    A. Preparation to build the tabernacle: God commands Moses to build Him a dwelling place.

        Points I will teach:
        1.

        2.

        3.

        4.

B. The offerings of the people and the workmen appointed:

1.

2.

3.

4.

C. The tabernacle:

1. **The fence and the gate:**

   i. What it did (function):

   ii. What it represents (symbolism):

2. **The brazen altar:**

   i. What it did (function):

   ii. What it represents (symbolism):

3. **The brazen laver:**

   i. What it did (function):

   ii. What it represents (symbolism):

4. **The table of showbread:**

   i. What it did (function):

   ii. What it represents (symbolism):

5. **The golden lampstand:**

   i. What it did (function):

ii. What it represents (symbolism):

6. **The altar of incense:**

   i. What it did (function):

   ii. What it represents (symbolism):

7. **The veil** between the Holy Place and the Holy of Holies:

   i. What it did (function):

   ii. What it represents (symbolism):

8. **The Ark of the Covenant:**

   i. What it did (function):

   ii. What it represents (symbolism):

9. **The presence of God filling the tabernacle**—how the cloud in the day and the pillar of fire in the night assured the people that God was with them and also directed their steps.

Part Three: The Application

Explain to your students that we are going to use the tabernacle as a guide or aide to us in spending some time with the Lord. If you'd like, share with them your own experience in trying this meditation. Invite your students to close their eyes and imagine they are walking through the tabernacle as you talk to them. Say to them:

1. First we are going to enter the gate and come to the bronze altar: *"Jesus, thank You that You are the door, that You made the way for me to come before the Father. Thank You that by Your blood I can enter the holy of holies and come before the very throne of God."* You might invite anyone who wants to thank Jesus for being our sacrifice to pray out loud using a loud voice for everyone to hear.

2. Now we are walking to the bronze laver where the priests washed their hands after making a sacrifice. Here we will examine our hearts for any sin that the Lord points out to us. Take a moment to ask the Lord if there is anything you need to confess to him and repent of. (Wait a minute or two in silence.) *"Thank You, Jesus, that Your blood washes us clean."*

3. Next we move into the holy place, and we see the candlestick, giving light to this room inside the tent of the tabernacle: This reminds us to invite the Holy Spirit to give us wisdom and revelation in

the knowledge of God. *"Father, may Your Spirit give us wisdom and revelation in the knowledge of Jesus. Teach us to know Your ways. We acknowledge that Your Word is a lamp to our feet and a light to our path. Help us to live by the light of Your word and the light of Your Spirit."*

4. Beside the candlestick, we see the table of showbread. The Word of God is as the bread of life to us who believe in Jesus. Let's use this time to meditate on our verse for today: "Have them make a sanctuary for me, and I will dwell among them." I'm going to speak some phrases, slowly. After I say a sentence, repeat it in your heart and think about what it means to you to know that God dwells with you and in you.

   Giving time for the students to think in between phrases, say:
   i. *Father, thank you that You want to dwell with us.*
   ii. *We love Your presence with us.*
   iii. *Spirit of God, You dwell within us.*
   iv. *We love You, Spirit of God.*
   v. *Father, we love You.*

   Depending on how well your students are engaging, you can repeat the phrases again or move on to the next point.

5. Next we come to the altar of incense where we can bring our prayers and intercession before the Lord. Let's pair up and take a few minutes to pray for each other. (Give them a minute to pair up). In every pair, I want one of you to put your hand up. Okay, good. Everyone with your hand up, you have one minute to tell your partner one prayer request. Ready? Go! (Time them for one minute). Okay, now the other person in each pair has one minute to pray for that request. Ready? Go! (Time them for one minute). Great! Now the person who was praying, you have one minute to tell your partner one prayer request. Ready? Go! (Time them for one minute). Okay, now the other person in each pair has one minute to pray for that request. Ready? Go! (Time them for one minute, then close in prayer).

Part Four: The Impact

A. Remind your students that God wants to dwell with them every moment of every day. This means that they can talk to Him all day long, whenever they want. It also means that God wants to share their day with them; He loves to listen to them talk about what they are doing and how they are feeling. Just like they get excited about something and can't wait to get home to tell Mom or Dad, they can share those same excited feelings with God. In fact, God desires them to tell Him! It's the same with hard or sad things in our life. God wants to share those times with us, too.

Remind your students that they never have to feel alone. God is always with them, indwelling them by the Holy Spirit. Just as God directed the Israelites in their travels, telling them when to go and when to stay, even so, God wants to direct our steps as well. The Israelites had to look at the tabernacle to see how God was directing each day. We only need to listen to God's still, small voice in our hearts. When we quiet our thoughts down and listen to God, He will speak to us. It is His delight!

Today we used the picture of the tabernacle to guide us in a time of fellowship with the Lord. If you want, you can use this pattern in your own quiet times with God. Many people do. One good thing about it is that it gives us a picture to focus on so that our thoughts don't wander. You don't have to come before God this way, but if it helps you, then use it as a tool. (If you use this picture often, you might share the impact it has had on your own life in God.)

Invite the children to join you in prayer

Father, thank You that You desire to dwell with Your people. Thank You that by Your Holy Spirit, You dwell within us today. You have made us to be Your tabernacle, Your dwelling place on earth. Help us to remember this every day. We love You! We want to learn how to dwell with You. We want to learn how to live each day with You, just as if You were walking by our side. By Your Holy Spirit, prompt our heart to speak to You throughout our day. Help us hear Your still, small voice telling us: Go this way, go that way. When we feel angry with someone, let us hear Your voice speaking peace to our hearts. When we feel like turning aside to sin, let us hear Your voice speaking faith and grace and courage to our hearts. Help us truly to live each day with You. So that You, Father, may be glorified in us through the name of Jesus, Amen.

B. End the class by encouraging your students to share with their family what they have learned today.
   1. Encourage students to share with their families their thoughts on God dwelling with us and in us.
   2. Encourage students to tell their families what they learned today about the tabernacle.
   3. Encourage them to consider asking if they can lead their family through the tabernacle one day this week.
   4. Encourage them to have their parents help them practice saying the five books of the Pentateuch and reciting the main events of Genesis and Exodus with the hand motions.
   5. Remind them about the at-home study pages at Forerunner Kids Club and encourage them to take a few minutes each day to work on them.

Questions to jump-start conversation with your 7- to 12-year-old on the way home from church:

1. I hear you learned about the tabernacle of Moses today. What was that?

2. Tell me what it looked like. Was there any furniture in the tabernacle? Like what?

3. Well, the Israelites were in a desert. Where did they get everything they needed to build the tabernacle?

Memory verse for this week:
> "Have them make a sanctuary for me, and I will dwell among them. Make this tabernacle and all its furnishings exactly like the pattern I will show you." (Ex. 25:8-9)

Key thoughts to remember:
1. God desired a place where He could dwell with His people and where they could meet to worship Him.
2. God gave specific instructions for this tabernacle because it is a picture about how He relates to us.

THEME: *The Pentateuch*

Lesson 9: *Exodus: Israel relates to God through the tabernacle*
Day One: Exodus 25:1-22

I. Read Exodus 25:1-22. As you do, answer the following:

    A. From whom will they take up an offering? Does every Israelite *have* to give?

    B. Although anyone can give who wants to, there are specific items they are looking for. What is God asking them to donate?

    C. What will they do with these items?

    D. Who will live in this tent-sanctuary?

    E. Can they make this any way that they want? How important is it that they follow the directions?

    F. What is the first item for which God gives them instructions?

    G. How big is the chest? Of what is made? With what do they overlay it?

    H. What do they make for carrying this chest?

    I. What goes on the cover?

    J. What goes inside this chest, this ark of the covenant?

II.   Think about these things and write down your thoughts.

    A. God says that He will dwell among the people, in this tabernacle. Other nations had temples where they kept their idol statues and went to worship their spirit gods. But they all believed that their gods lived high above and far away from them. What do you think the Israelites felt when they heard that their God would live with them, in their midst, that He would speak to them from the space between the cherubim on the ark?

    B. How do you feel knowing that God dwells with you all the time and is with you every moment of the day?

    C. Why do you think God gave the directions for the ark of the covenant first? (Hint: verse 22)

THEME: *The Pentateuch*

Lesson 9: *Exodus: Israel relates to God through the tabernacle*
Day Two: Exodus 25:23-40

I. Read Exodus 25:23-40. As you do, answer the following:

    A. What is the second piece of furniture for which God gives instructions?

    B. How big is it? Of what is made? With what do they overlay it?

    C. What do they make for carrying this table?

    D. What kinds of items did they make to use with this table and the offerings? Of what are they made?

    E. What will be put on the table?

    F. What is the third piece of furniture? Of what is it made?

    G. What flower adorns this piece?

    H. What else did they make to use with the lampstand?

    I. How much gold did they use?_____ (That's about seventy-five pounds. In the past twenty years, gold has cost from about $400 to almost $1,000 per ounce. Have your parent help you figure out how much seventy pounds would cost.)

Here's a picture of the lampstand from the time of Jesus:

II.   Think about these things and write down your thoughts.

    A. God commanded that loaves of bread be made daily and placed on the table. What did Jesus say about bread in Matthew 4:4? In John 6:35 and 48-51?

    B. The lampstand was the only source of light in the tabernacle. What did Jesus say about the light in John 8:12?

At-Home Daily Activity Sheet 3

THEME: *The Pentateuch*

Lesson 9: *Exodus: Israel relates to God through the tabernacle*
Day Three: Exodus 26

I. Read Exodus 26. This chapter is about the curtains and wood frames that used to construct the actual tabernacle itself. Here is a picture of what the tabernacle looked like. As you read, look at the picture to identify what part of the tent you are reading about.

1. What picture is embroidered or woven into the curtains?

2. How are all the curtains hung together to make this large tent structure?

3. In verse 6, what metal is used to make the clasp fasteners for the inner part of the tabernacle?

4. In verse 11, what metal is used to make the clasp fasteners for the outer part of the tabernacle?

5. In verse 14, what materials are used to make the tabernacle waterproof?

6. Notice that the frame is made of acacia wood. These are frames, not solid pieces, since they are fifteen feet tall and two and a half feet wide, yet the acacia tree trunk is not that wide. With what are the frames overlaid?

7. What color is the curtain that separates the holy place from holy of holies where the ark was kept? What was embroidered into this curtain?

8. What color is the curtain that is the entrance to the tabernacle?

II.   Think about these things and write down your thoughts.
   1.   These are very detailed instructions: fifty of this, eleven of that, loops on this end of the curtain, etc. What does Hebrews 8:5 tell us about why the instructions were so detailed and why Moses had to follow them exactly?

   2.   Jesus told us that now we are free from worshipping God in one particular place and that what God desires are those who worship Him in spirit and in truth. How do you feel about this?

At-Home Daily Activity Sheet 4

THEME: *The Pentateuch*

Lesson 9: *Exodus: Israel relates to God through the tabernacle*
Day Four: Exodus 27:1-8

I. Read Exodus 271-8. As you do, answer the following:

   A. What is the fourth piece of furniture?

   B. How big is it? _____ tall and _____ wide (that's about seven and a half feet wide and deep; about four and a half feet tall)

   C. Look at verses 1 and 8. Is it solid?

   D. What are they supposed to make at each top corner?

   E. With what metal are they told to cover it?

   F. How will it be carried?

   G. Notice in verse 4 that they are to make a grating for it, a bronze network. This is to allow the burnt ashes to fall through, and to allow air underneath so that the sacrifices will burn well. So the poles are used not only to carry the altar, but also to lift it so that they can clean out the ashes. What did they make in verse 3 to help them clean out the ashes?

   H. What other items did they make in verse 3?

   I. What are all these utensils made of?

Note: Bronze is made by mixing copper and tin. Bronze has a prophetic interpretation of judgment, while gold represents deity and royalty.

II.   Think about these things and write down your thoughts.

   A. Why do you think that this altar was covered in bronze when all the other items in the tabernacle were covered in gold?

   B. Horns represented authority and strength. In many sacrifices, the priest was to sprinkle the blood on the horns. What do you think this represented?

THEME: *The Pentateuch*

Lesson 9: *Exodus: Israel relates to God through the tabernacle*
Day Five: Exodus 30:1-10 and 17-21

I. Read Exodus 30:1-10 and 17-21 and answer the following:
 1. What is the fifth piece of furniture?

 2. How big is it? _____ tall and _____ wide (that's about one and a half feet wide and deep; about three feet tall)

 3. Look at verses 1 and 8. Is it solid?

 4. What are they supposed to make at each top corner?

 5. With what metal are they told to cover it?

 6. How will it be carried?

 7. Where is it placed in the tabernacle?

 8. What is burned on it?

 9. Can any other things be burned on it for other offerings?

Note: once a year, on the Day of Atonement, the high priest anoints the horns with the blood from the national sacrifice to represent the cleansing of the sins of the nation, making their incense of prayer acceptable to God.

 10. In verse 17, what is the last piece of furniture?

 11. Why do you think it is made of bronze and not gold?

 12. Who is to use it? What are they to wash?

First Quarter, Year One: Biblical Foundations for Children
Lesson Ten:
Intro to the Pentateuch: Leviticus

Lesson Objective: to introduce the student to the book of Leviticus.

Scope of lessons on Leviticus—three lessons consisting of:
1. Intro to the book of Leviticus; Israel relates to God through the priests
2. Israel relates to God through the sacrifices
3. Israel relates to God through the feasts

Biblical Foundation: Background information on the book of Leviticus:

I. Meaning of the name and authorship:

    a. Name in English: Leviticus. It comes from the Greek. It means "relating to the Levites" and refers to all the religious instructions given in the book. The descendants of Levi, called the Levites, were in charge of the tabernacle and all things religious. The priests were descendants of Aaron, who was also a descendant of Levi.

    b. The name in Hebrew: "The Lord Spoke," which is the first few words of the book in Hebrew. It is very appropriate since much of the book contains direct commands spoken by the Lord. Jewish rabbis also refer to it as "the Priests' Manual" since it describes all the duties of the priests.

    c. Author: Moses. He wrote most of it during the years that Israel wandered in the desert. As the book was copied, year after year, some updates were written to reflect current place names, etc.

II. Purpose of the book: to describe the offerings and feasts and record them for future generations of the Israelites. Also to record more laws in the arena of code of conduct.

III. Outline of Leviticus

    A. Worship and sacrifices (ch. 1-16)
        i. Five kinds of sacrifices (ch. 1-7)
        ii. The ordination and work of Israel's priests (ch. 8-10)
        iii. Instructions for cleanliness and holiness (11-16)

    B. A holy lifestyle (ch. 17-27)
        i. Laws for all Israel (ch. 17-20)
        ii. Laws for the priests (ch. 21-22)
        iii. Seven festivals (ch. 23)
        iv. Additional laws, penalties, and blessings (ch. 24-27)

II.   The Levitical priesthood
  A. Aaron and his descendants were appointed as the only priests—Exodus 28:1.
      Here the Lord said that from among the Israelites, only Aaron and his sons were to serve
      the Lord as priests, and Aaron as the high priest.
      1. Exodus 29 describes how Aaron and his sons were to be consecrated to the Lord
          through animal sacrifice.
      2. Special clothing was also prescribed for them, and the special garments of the high
          priest were to pass from father to son over the generations.
      3. In Leviticus 10, two of Aaron's four sons used unauthorized fire to light the incense
          in their censers, and the Lord struck them dead. They had been instructed only to
          use the fire that had been kindled by the fire that came out from the presence of
          God when they had made the offering to dedicate the priests. Nadab and Abihu died
          in this manner, so all the priest of Israel were descended from Eleazar and Ithamar.
  B. The Levites were appointed to serve in the tabernacle in practical ways—Numbers 1:50-53.
      Here the Lord instructed that the tabernacle and its furniture were to be moved only by the
      Levites. They would take it down when the Israelites were to break camp, and they would
      set it up when the nation made camp. Moreover, as a tribe, they were to set up their own
      tents surrounding the tabernacle, as a buffer zone between the presence of God and the rest
      of the Israelites.
      1. The Levites became consecrated to God in place of all the firstborn of the rest of
          Israel (Numbers 3:11-13).
      2. God gave each clan of the Levites a specific task or tasks to do (Numbers 3; 4).
  C. The Israelites could not approach God directly. They had to come to God through the
      ministry of the priesthood.
      1. Only the priests could slay the animal sacrifices.
      2. Only the priests could offer the sacrifices on the bronze altar.
      3. Only the priests could offer the incense.
      4. Only the priests could enter the holy place.
      5. Only the high priest could enter the holy of holies, and only once a year.
      6. The only things a normal Israelite could do would be to pray, to sing worship songs,
          and to dance before the Lord.
  D. Jesus came as a priest of the line of Melchizedek; He is a better priest.
      1.   He is greater than the Levitical priests because Levi, through Abraham, gave tithes
          to Melchizedek (Hebrews chapters 5-7).
      2. I Timothy 2:5 explains that we no longer need a priest on earth as a mediator
          between God and man, but that Jesus the God-man is the only mediator now
          between God and man.
      3. He offered a better sacrifice than the sacrifices of the Levitical priesthood (Heb.
          7:27; 9:12).
      4. The Levitical high priest had to offer sacrifice for his own sins (Heb. 5:3) but Jesus
          did not.

THEME: *The Pentateuch*

Lesson 10: *Introduction to Leviticus*

Part One: The Invitation

A. Review:
  1. Unit theme: God is a Father who desires a family.

  2. Lead your students in reciting the names of the five books of the Pentateuch.

  3. Lead your students in reciting the main events of Genesis and Exodus, with hand motions:

Creation	Abraham	Moses	Red Sea
Fall	Isaac	"Let my people go!"	Mt. Sinai
Flood	Jacob	"No!"	10 Commandments
Tower of Babel	Joseph	Ten Plagues	tabernacle
Nations scatter	To Egypt	Passover	

B. Introduce today's lesson topic and explain that in this book, God gave the Israelites more commands about how to relate to Him and to each other.

C. Share the key verse for this lesson with your students: "The Lord said to Moses, 'Speak to the entire assembly of Israel and say to them: Be a holy and set-apart people because I, the Lord your God, am holy." (Lev. 19:1-2)

D. Invite your students to join you on the journey of hearing from God through the book of Leviticus.

Part Two: The Impartation

I. Introduce the third book of the Pentateuch: Leviticus

 A. Ask your students to turn to Leviticus 1. Read chapter 1:1.

  1. Explain the name of the book in Hebrew and English.

  2. Talk about the author of the book and when he wrote it.

3. Explain the purpose of the book.

4. Share the outline of the book.

  i. Worship and sacrifices (ch. 1-16)
      1. Five kinds of sacrifices (ch. 1-7)
      2. The ordination and work of Israel's priests (ch. 8-10)
      3. Instructions for cleanliness and holiness (11-16)

  ii. A holy lifestyle (ch. 17-27)
      1. Laws for all Israel (ch. 17-20)
      2. Laws for the priests (ch. 21-22)
      3. Seven festivals (ch. 23)
      4. Additional laws, penalties, and blessings (ch. 24-27)

After this, teach the motions for the following events (hand and arm motions are given in the appendix):
        Priests
        Five sacrifices
        Seven festivals
        Holy living

Have students stand and practice the motions while saying the events (in order). Give plenty of time for students to learn it well. Once they know it pretty well, add it to the motions for Genesis and Exodus.

B. Teach about the Levitical priesthood

  1. Introduce the Levites:

      a. Who they were:

      b. What they did:

2. Introduce the Priests:

   a. Who they were:

   b. What they did:

   c. The high priest and what he did:

3. Talk about the function of the priests in terms of being a mediator between God and man.

   a. How the Levites' tents surrounded the tabernacle as a "buffer zone."

   b. How a regular Israelite had to have a priest offer a sacrifice on his behalf to atone for his sin.

4. Compare the Levitical priesthood to the priesthood of Jesus in the order of Melchizedek.

   a. Jesus is a perfect high priest.

   b. Jesus offered a better sacrifice.

   c. Jesus opened the way for us into the Holy of Holies.

   d. Jesus is the only mediator between God and man: He himself is the God-man.

   e. The Levitical priesthood was a picture for us to use to understand what Jesus did in offering himself for us. Next week we will study the sacrifices to see how they give us understanding into different aspects of Jesus.

Part Three: The Application

A. Lead your students back into worship. Begin with the song, "Take me in to the Holy of Holies." You might also sing, "Come into the Holy of Holies / Worship by the blood of the Lamb." Use these to lead into several songs that focus our worship on the Lord. You might also sing, "Holiness, holiness is what I long for / Holiness is what I need . . . " and "Holiness unto the Lord, unto the King . . . "

B. At the end of your worship time, ask your students to share how they feel when they worship. Then ask them how they think they would feel if they had to have a priest help them to communicate with God.

Part Four: The Impact

A. Explain to your students that God still desires His people to live holy lives. Thankfully, God no longer expects us to keep many of the cultural laws which He gave the Israelites, especially the laws about what they could and couldn't eat, or what made a person unclean in the eyes of God. Through the blood of Jesus we have been washed clean. God still wants us to live holy lives by letting His Holy Spirit work holiness in our hearts. The fruit of the Spirit at work in our hearts is a faithful lifestyle that treats other people with love, that is full of joy and peace, that has patience for other people, that is full of goodness, that treats other people with gentleness, that responds with meekness, and that is self-controlled. When we let the Holy Spirit work in us so that we respond with godliness, then we are being holy as God is holy. Lead your students in prayer, having them repeat each sentence after you:

Father, thank You that the blood of Jesus washes me from all my sin. Thank You that I don't need a priest to offer sacrifices for me because the sacrifice of Jesus was enough. Thank You that I can come directly to Your throne of grace to find help whenever I need it. Father, I want to be holy as You are holy. Holy Spirit, please do a work of holiness in my heart. Give me grace to respond rightly to people in my life. Work the fruit of the Spirit in me. I say to You today that I choose holiness. I want to live a holy life for Your glory. I want to be set apart for You. I don't want to value what the world values. I want to value what You value. I want to see things the way that You do. I want to be holy as You are holy. Pour out Your grace upon me. Give me great grace. Give me abundant grace. Help me to please You. So that You would receive glory through my life. I love You, Father-God! We love You, and we come to You in the name of Jesus, Amen!

B. Close by encouraging your students to share with their family what they have learned today.
   1. Suggest that they share the theme of the book of Leviticus with their family this afternoon. Encourage them to have their parents help them practice reciting the main events of Genesis, Exodus, and Leviticus with the hand motions.
   2. Encourage students to tell their families what they learned today about the priesthood.
   3. Remind them about the at-home study pages at Forerunner Kids Club and encourage them to take a few minutes each day to work on them.

CAR TALK

Questions to jump-start conversation with your 7- to 12-year-old on the way home from church:

1. What does the word *Leviticus* mean?

2. Why is that the name for the third book of the Bible? What happened in that book?

3. What do you remember the most about today's lesson?

4. How do you feel when you worship God?

Memory Verse for this week:

> "The Lord said to Moses, 'Speak to the entire assembly of Israel and say to them: Be a holy and set-apart people because I, the Lord your God, is holy." (Lev. 19:1-2)

THEME: *The Pentateuch*

Lesson 10: *Introduction to Leviticus*
Day One: The Priests

Here is a sample page from a Bible concordance. A concordance lists words in the Bible alphabetically and gives all the verses in which that word is used. This is a partial listing for the words *priest* and *priests*:

Priest, Priests

Gen.14:18		He was *p* of God Most High
Ex.	28:1	minister to me in the *p* office
	28:41	minister to me in the *p* office
	29:1	minister to me in the *p* office
	29:9	the *p* office shall be
	29:44	minister to me in the *p* office
	39: 14	to minister in the *p* office
Lev.	1:7	the sons of Aaron the *p*
	1:12	the *p* shall
	1:15	the *p* shall bring
	2:2	Aaron's sons the *p*
	2:2	the *p* shall burn
	13:9	brought to the *p*
	14:13	offering is the *p*
Deut.	20: 2	the *p* shall approach
	26:3	go to the *p*
Josh.21:13		Aaron the *p* they gave Hebron
2 Kgs.	16:11	the *p* built
2 Kgs.	22:8	the high *p* said

Use the verse references above to answer the questions. If you have any trouble, talk with your parents.

1. List some duties of the priests.

2. What should Moses do to set apart or sanctify the priest?

3. Who will be the priests?

4. For how long will they be priests?

5. Other than Moses, who else will sanctify the priests?

6. Which city was given to the priests to be a city of refuge?

7. Which priest met with Abraham?

At-Home Daily Activity Sheet 2

THEME: *The Pentateuch*

Lesson 10: *Introduction to Leviticus*
Day Two: Jesus and the priesthood

Here is another sample page from a Bible concordance. This is a partial listing for the word *priest*.

Heb 2:17   faithful high *p* in service to God
  3: 1   and high *p* whom we confess
  4: 14   have a great high *p* who has gone
   15   do not have a high *p* who is unable
  5: 1   every high *p* taken from among
   5 of becoming a high p
   6 you are a *p* forever
   10 of God a high *p* after the order
  6: 20   he has become a high *p* forever
  7: 1   *p* of the most high God who met
   3 Son of God her main a *p* forever
   11 *p* should rise after the order
   15 arises another *p*

Heb 7: 16   become a *p* not on the basis of
Heb 7: 20   not without an oath was he made *p*
   26 such a high *p* meets our need
   27 unlike other high *p*, he does not
  8: 1   We do have such a high *p*
   3 for every high *p* is ordained to
   4 on earth he should not be a *p*
  9: 7   went the high *p* alone once every
   11 came as a high *p* of the good
   25 the high *p* enters the Most Holy
  10: 11   Day after day every *p* stands
   21 a great *p* over the house of God
  13: 11   The high *p* carries the blood

Use these concordance references to study the priesthood of Jesus:

1.   From where do high priests come?

2.   How did Jesus become a priest?

3.   Was Jesus part of the Levitical priesthood, of the order of Aaron?

4.   Of what order was He a priest?

5.   For how long is He a priest?

6.   What do other high priest need to do that Jesus does *not* need to do?

7.   Where did the high priest go every year?

8.   Why is Jesus the right high priest for us?

9. After Jesus made His sacrifice, where did He sit down?

10. How does the priesthood of Jesus compare to the Old Testament priesthood? List some similarities and some differences:

Similarities:

Differences:

CHILDREN'S EQUIPPING CENTER

THEME: *The Pentateuch*

Lesson 10: *Introduction to Leviticus*
Day Three: Moses in the New Testament

We've been studying about Moses in the Old Testament. We can use a concordance to find out what the New Testament has to say about him.

Moses

Mt.	8:	4	Offer the gift *M* commanded
	17:	3	*M* and Elijah appeared to them
		4	One for you, one for *M*, and one
	19:	7	did *M* command that a man
		8	*M* permitted you to
	22:	24	*M* said, "If a man die, having no
Mk.	7:	10	*M* said, "Honor your father and
	12:	26	have you not read in the book of M
Lk.	2:	22	the law of M were accomplished
	5:	14	according as the law of M commanded
Jn.	1:	17	For the law was given by M, but
	3:	14	as M lifted up the serpent in the
	5:	45	you, even M in whom you trust
		46	For had you believed M, you would
	6:	32	M gave you not bread from

Acts	3:	22	For M truly said to the fathers
	7:20		in which time M was born, and
		22	M was learned in all the wisdom
		29	Then M fled
		31	When M saw it, he wondered
Rom	5:14		death reigned from Adam to M
	9:15		He said to M, "I will have mercy
	10:	5	M describes the righteousness
1 Co	10:	2	All baptized into M in the cloud
2 Co	3:	7	not steadfastly behold the face of M
		13	like M who put a veil over his
Heb	3:	3	worthy of more glory than M
Jude		9	disputed about the body of M
Rev	15:	3	sing the song of M the servant of God

Use these concordance references to study about Moses in the New Testament:

1. Did Moses ever set foot on earth in the New Testament?

2. Who told the whole story of Moses in his evangelistic sermon?

3. How do we know that Jesus believed that Moses wrote the book of Exodus?

4. Are any of Moses' songs sung in heaven??

5. To what story about Moses did Jesus compare His death on the cross?

6. Why did Joseph and Mary take Jesus to the temple to present him to the Lord?

7. Who fought about the body of Moses when he died?

8. What sacrifices did Jesus command the leper to offer after Jesus healed him?

9. In what way are we not like Moses, according to Paul?

At-Home Daily Activity Sheet 4

THEME: *The Pentateuch*

Lesson 10: *Introduction to Leviticus*
Day Four: On-line concordance

Do this activity with a parent supervising you or working with you.

On the internet, point your browser to:
 www.biblestudytools.com/Concordances/StrongsExhaustiveConcordance/

Type the word Aaron in the place marked "search for."
In the place marked "in" choose "whole Bible."
Then click on "Find."

You should find about 330 entries for "Aaron." You can scroll down through the ones on the page. When you click on "next 20" you will get the next twenty entries.

Answer the following questions about Aaron:

1. Give references from three different New Testament books about Aaron:

    a.

    b.

    c.

2. What does the book of Micah tell us about Aaron?

3. In the book of Ezra, who was the descendant of Aaron who left Babylon and went to Jerusalem during the reign of Artaxerxes?

4. Whom did Nehemiah direct should be with the Levites when they collect the tithes?

5. Which descendant of Aaron served as high priest in the book of Judges?

THEME: *The Pentateuch*

Lesson 10: *Introduction to Leviticus*
Day Five: Concordance study

Today, you may use a concordance if your family owns one, or the on-line concordance. Talk about this with your parent and get their permission first.

Think of a word, topic, or person that interests you in the Bible. Look up the word or name and read some Bible verses about it.

Write down what you learn:

First Quarter, Year One: Biblical Foundations for Children
Lesson Eleven:
Leviticus: Israel Relates to God through the Sacrifices

Objective: To introduce the student to the Old Testament sacrificial system and the prophetic pictures of Jesus' sacrifice in them.

Key verse for this lesson: "These are the regulations for the burnt offering, the grain offering, the sin offering, the guilt offering, the ordination offering, and the fellowship offering." (Lev. 7:37)

Key thoughts to consider and to pass on:
1. God set up the sacrificial system as a means for the people of God to atone for their sin, fellowship with Him, and give offerings to Him until Jesus made His sacrifice once for all.
2. God gave specific instructions for the sacrifices because they are a picture about Jesus and His sacrifice for us.

Review from last week:

Outline of Leviticus

I. Worship and sacrifices (ch. 1-16)
    1. Five kinds of sacrifices (ch. 1-7)
    2. The ordination and work of Israel's priests (ch. 8-10)
    3. Instructions for cleanliness and holiness (11-16)

II. A holy lifestyle (ch. 17-27)
    1. Laws for all Israel (ch. 17-20)
    2. Laws for the priests (ch. 21-22)
    3. Seven festivals (ch. 23)
    4. Additional laws, penalties, and blessings (ch. 24-27)

Biblical Foundation

I. **Journaling through Leviticus 1-7.**

    A. Read Leviticus 1:1-2. The Lord says, "When you bring an offering . . ."

        1. Is God commanding them to bring an offering, or is He giving them instructions about a practice with which they are familiar?

        2. Did their forefathers sacrifice to the Lord?

3. Did God ever give Abraham or Isaac or Jacob detailed instructions about sacrificing to Him?

B. Why do you think the Lord is doing this at this time? Do you think it is a part of the system of the Mosaic covenant?

C. What is the designation for this first type of offering?

    1. What may be offered as a burnt offering?

        a. Verse 3:
        b. Verse 10:
        c. Verse 14:

    2. In verse 4, what do you learn about this offering?

    3. Who slaughters it?

    4. What does the priest do?

    5. How much of it is to be burned?

D. In chapter 2, what type of offering is described?

    1. What two kinds of grain offerings are there?

        a. Verse 1:
        b. Verse 4:

    2. With a grain offering, how much of it is to be burned?

    3. What happens to the rest?

        a. In verses 3 and 10, how does the Lord describe this part of the offering?

        b. Why do you think He calls the part that the priests eat "a most holy part of the offerings to the Lord"?

    4. In verse 11, what regulation does the Lord give concerning the grain offering?

    5. In verse 13, what other regulation does He give concerning the grain offering?

E. In chapter 3, what offering is described?

   1. What three animals may be offered? (verse 1, 7, 12)

   2. From verses 3 and 4, what parts are burned in the fire?

   3. What do you think happens with the rest of the animal?

   4. So why do you think this is called a fellowship offering? How do you think the person making the offering is fellowshipping with God through it?

F. What type of offering is described in chapter 4?

   1. 4:2, 13, 22, 27—one word is repeated concerning the sin: "unintentionally." So is this an offering for rebellious sin, or for sin because we are human and imperfect?

   2. 4:3,14, 25—what type of offering does God call this?

   3. Different people or groups of people are described, with different animals to be offered as a sin offering. For each, list what they offer:

      a. An anointed priest:

      b. The whole community:

      c. A community leader:

      d. A community member: a _____ or a _____

Note: with the offering for the priest or for the community, the blood is brought into the tabernacle itself and is used to anoint the altar of incense. This symbolizes cleaning the priest or the nation so that intercession may be restored.

G. Chapter 5 describes a similar offering, a guilt offering. Under what circumstances is a guilt offering required?

   1. Verse 1:

   2. Verse 2:

   3. Verse 3:

   4. Verse 4:

H. What may be offered as a guilt offering?

    1. Verse 5:

    2. Verse 7:

    3. Verse 11:

    4. Under what conditions may these substitutes be made?

I. 5:15-16 describes a special sin. What is the sin, and what offering is made to atone for it? How does this offering differ from the other guilt offerings?

J. What type of sin is described in verse 17?

K. What must be brought as an offering?

L. What type of sin is described in 6:1-3?

    1. Is this an unintentional or intentional sin?

    2. When you read, "or if he commits any such sin that people may do, when he thus sins and becomes guilty . . . " do you think God is describing a rebellious heart or a fallen human being? Why do you think that?

M. Verses 4-5: what must he do in addition to bringing his guilt offering?

N. When must he do this?

O. How does Jesus refer to this in Matthew 5:23-24?

P. Leviticus 6:8-13 give specific regulations concerning how the priests are to maintain the brazen altar and the burnt offerings.

    1. Are the sacrifices and ashes taken from the altar at the end of each day?

    2. What must the priest wear to take the ashes from the altar and place them beside the altar

    3. What must he wear to move the ashes from beside the altar to a place outside the camp?

4. Why do you think God wanted him to wear his priestly garments to move the ashes from the altar to the floor? What does that communicate to the priest and to the people?

5. Why do you think the ashes had to be placed in an area that was ceremonially clean? After all, it was just ashes. What do you think God was saying—that they couldn't be dumped in the unclean areas outside the camp (like the latrine areas, or the "bury the dead animals" areas)?

Q. In verse 9, 12, and 13, God repeats a phrase, a command. What is it?

1. Why do you think this was so important?

2. Do you know how the flame was lit in the first place? If not, go to Leviticus 9:24.

3. So what was it that made this fire so important?

4. What do you think it represented? (See Acts 2:3)

5. How much of the grain offering is burned on the altar?

R. Verses 14-23 give specific regulations concerning the priests and the grain offerings.

1. What happens to the rest of it?

2. Where may they eat it?

3. What are the restrictions on how they prepare it?

4. Who may eat of it?

5. Are the priests supposed to make grain offerings themselves?

6. Who prepares it?

7. Do they eat of this one or burn it all?

8. From where do you think the priests get the flour and oil for their own offering?

S. Verses 24-10 gives specific regulations concerning the priests and the sin offerings.

1. We learned in Leviticus 4 that with a sin offering for a leader or a normal person, the priest anoints the altar with the blood, then burns the fat, the kidneys, and the

covering of the liver. However, he does not burn the meat. Who may eat of it according to Leviticus 6:26 & 29?

2.   Where must it be eaten?

3.   What are the regulations concerning cooking it?

Note: verse 30 says that any sin offering whose blood is brought into the tabernacle may not be eaten. In Leviticus 4, this refers to the sin offering for a priest and the sin offering for the nation.

T. Leviticus 7:1-10 gives specific regulations concerning the priests and the guilt offerings.

1.   What is burned?

2.   Who gets the meat from this type of sacrifice?

3.   According to verse 8, what else may the officiating priest keep? Why is this important to him?

4.   Which kind of grain offering belongs to the officiating priest?

5.   Which kind of grain offering is divided among the priests?

U. Verses 11-34 gives specific regulations concerning the priests and the fellowship offerings.

1.   What are two of the reasons why a person would offer a fellowship offering?

   a.   Verse 12:

   b.   Verse 16:

2.   If the offering is prompted by thanksgiving:

   a.   What must the person offer in addition to the animal?

   b.   How many kinds?

   c.   Who eats them?

   d.   By when must the meat be eaten?

3.   If the offering is prompted by the end of a vow or is a freewill offering:

       a. How long does one have to eat it all?

       b. Is it necessary to bring bread?

       c. What must be done with any meat leftover?

    4. Since the meat of a fellowship offering can be eaten by the ordinary person who brings the offering and by his family, what restrictions does God place on who may eat it or may not? (Verses 19-21)

V. In verses 22-27, what does God command concerning the fat and the blood of animals?

W. In every other offering, the priest brings the fat to the altar. In verses 29-30, what does God command concerning the fellowship offering?

Here is what happens: the man who wishes to make a fellowship offering brings the animal to the entrance to the tabernacle. He puts his hand on its head, so that it symbolizes the giving of himself, and then he slays the animal. The priest catches some of the blood to sprinkle on the sides of the altar. The man cuts out the fat, the kidneys, and liver, and brings them to the altar. The priest takes them from him, puts them on the altar, and they are burned. The man cuts out the part of the animal from which we would make chuck steak and chuck roast; he cuts it out as one large piece, and he waves it in front of the altar. Then it is given to Aaron and his sons, to be divided among them. Next the man cuts out another piece, perhaps from the right thigh, perhaps a brisket, or perhaps the area where we get sirloin steak or bottom and top round steaks, and he gives this to the priest who is officiating at his sacrifice. All the rest of the meat is his, but must be eaten that day. If he brings a cow, most likely he will share it with his entire extended family or with his neighbors. Hence, he fellowships with God and with his family and friends. If he offers a lamb or a goat, there is less meat to share around, but still enough to feed and fellowship with quite a few people!

X. Verses 35-36: Why are the priests allowed to eat part of the offerings?

II. Symbolism in the Sacrifices

A. The burnt offering:

    1. A male without defect: symbolizes Jesus, who is without sin.

    2. The one who offers the sacrifice lays his hand on the head of the offering and it is accepted on his behalf: symbolizes Jesus who took our place

    3. It makes atonement: Jesus made atonement for our sins. Atonement means making reparations for a wrong done. The derivation of the word is from the old English word *onement,* meaning "unity," plus the Latin prefix *ad-,* indicating "towards." In simple terms, the atonement makes us "at one" with God; it restores unity of relationship.

4. In the area of atonement, the burnt offering is the only sacrifice that atones for sin committed knowingly, intentionally. It is the only sacrifice that restores relationship with God when the rebellious heart repents.
5. The sacrificial animals as types or symbols:
    a. The bull or ox: symbolizes Jesus as the servant.
    b. The sheep or lamb: symbolizes the one who is led quietly to be slaughtered (Isa. 53:7).
    c. The goat: symbolizes the sinner, as in the parable of the sheep and the goats (Mt. 25:31-46). Here, the picture is Jesus taking on our sin and "becoming sin for us."
    d. The dove or pigeon: in the sacrificial system, symbolizes poverty, since it is the offering given by the poor. Jesus emptied himself and became poor on our behalf. Also symbolizes our poverty before the Lord.

B. The grain offering:
1. Symbolizes Jesus, who said, "I am the bread of life." (John 6:48)
2. Oil symbolizes the presence of the Holy Spirit.
3. Incense symbolizes His intercession for us and the pleasant fragrance of His life towards God (2 Cor. 2:14-15).
4. Salt both counters the effect of yeast and preserves; Jesus spoke of the believer as the salt of the earth. Salt is also used in healing, as when we soak an infected part in salt water.
5. Yeast symbolizes sin and false teaching. There was to be *no* yeast in the grain offering.
6. Honey symbolizes the flesh. There was to be *no* honey in the grain offering.

Note: the combination of yeast and honey causes dough to rise, to be inflated. The yeast feeds on the honey and gives off a chemical gas caused by fermentation, which leads to the dough being inflated. In the grain offering, the picture is that we don't want to present our flesh and our sin, which feed off each other to inflate us.

C. The fellowship offering:
1. In this offering, God is given a part, the priesthood is given a part, the officiating priest is given a part, and the worshipper is given a part to share with his family and friends. Everyone fellowships together through the "meal" they share.
2. This offering is given in thanksgiving for what God has done, or at the completion of a sacred vow (such as a Nazarite vow), or simply as a freewill offering.
3. As this is not an offering for atonement, sin, or guilt, it is the only sacrifice of which the worshipper may eat.

D. The sin offering:
1. This offering deals with sin committed unintentionally. Notice that while the sin was committed unintentionally, God points out the guilt of the one who committed it. Personal responsibility is stressed, even when one is unaware of breaking a command.
2. In making the offering, the guilty person had to lay his hand on the head of the

animal, thus acknowledging that the animal was to die in his place. Next, he had to kill the animal himself, stressing the personal responsibility. His sin caused the death of that animal.

3. Notice that the greater one's sphere of authority, the larger or more expensive an animal he had to offer for his sin. Compare this to James 3:1, where James tells us that those who teach will be judged more carefully or more in-depth than those who do not.

    a. Notice that the offering for the sin of the high priest is the same as for the sin of the whole nation. Very often the high priest set the direction for the entire nation, particularly during the times when there was no king.

    b. Community leaders brought a male goat, symbolizing authority over others.

    c. Community members brought a female goat or lamb, symbolizing being one who was led.

E. The guilt offering:

1. This offering deals with guilt in the specific areas of touching something unclean, failing to speak up to testify for or against someone who has been publicly charged when one has been witness to the situation, or making an oath thoughtlessly and not keeping it ("Mom, I promise I'll clean my room later! Honest, I promise I will . . . ").

III. Reflect upon the sacrifice of Jesus, the better sacrifice

1. "He did not enter by means of the blood of goats and calves; but he entered the Most Holy Place once for all by his own blood, having obtained eternal redemption. The blood of goats and bulls and the ashes of a heifer sprinkled on those who are ceremonially unclean sanctify them so that they are outwardly clean. How much more then, will the blood of Christ, who through the eternal Spirit offered himself unblemished to God, cleanse our consciences from acts that lead to death so that we may serve the living God!" (Heb. 9:12-14)

2. 'Nor did he enter heaven to offer himself again and again, the way the high priest enters the Most Holy Place every year with blood that is not his own. Then Christ would have had to suffer many times since the creation of the world. But now he has appeared once for all at the end of the ages to do away with sin by the sacrifice of himself." (Heb. 9:25-26)

3. "We have been made holy through the sacrifice of the body of Jesus Christ once for all. Day after day every priest stands and performs his religious duties; again and again he offers the same sacrifices, which can never take away sins. But when this priest, Jesus, had offered for all time one sacrifice for sins, he sat down at the right hand of God. Since that time he waits for his enemies to be made his footstool, because by one sacrifice he has made perfect forever those who are being made holy." (Heb. 10: 10-14)

4. "And where sins have been forgiven, there is no longer any sacrifice for sin. Therefore, brothers, since we have confidence to enter the Most Holy Place by the blood of Jesus, by a new and living way opened for us through the curtain, that is, his body, and since we have a great priest over the house of God, let us draw near to God with a sincere heart in full assurance of faith, having our hearts sprinkled to cleanse us from a guilty conscience and having our bodies washed with pure water." (Heb. 10:18-22)

B. Finish these sentences:

1. The sacrifice that impacted me the most was _____ because . . .

2. What thrilled me the most about the sacrificial system was . . .

3. What bothered me the most about the sacrificial system was . . .

4. If I had been going to worship God at the tabernacle, and had to get in line with my little lamb sacrifice, hearing the animals' cries, seeing the blood, smelling all the smells, I would have felt . . .

5. The fellowship offering, where everyone shared the meal together . . .

6. When I read about Jesus offering a better sacrifice, I thought . . .

Lesson Presentation outline template

THEME: *The Pentateuch*
Lesson 11: *Leviticus: Israel relates to God through the Sacrifices*

Part One: The Invitation

A. Review:

    1. Unit theme: God is a Father who desires a family.

    2. Lead your students in reciting the names of the five books of the Pentateuch.

    3. Lead your students in reciting the main events of Genesis, Exodus, and Leviticus, with hand motions:

Creation	Abraham	Moses	Red Sea
Fall	Isaac	"Let my people go!"	Mt. Sinai
Flood	Jacob	"NO!"	10 Commandments
Tower of Babel	Joseph	Ten Plagues	tabernacle
Nations scatter	To Egypt	Passover	

Priests
Five sacrifices
Seven festivals
Holy Living

B. Introduce today's lesson topic and explain that God gave the Israelites instructions about how to make sacrifices to Him so that they could be restored to fellowship with Him after they sinned.

C. Share the key verse for this lesson with your students: "These are the regulations for the burnt offering, the grain offering, the sin offering, the guilt offering, the ordination offering, and the fellowship offering." (Lev. 7:37)

Explain that there were five sacrifices, that each had their own purpose, and that today we are going to learn about those sacrifices and how we can see Jesus through the pictures that they make.

D. Invite your students to meet with God and His desire for relationship with them through the sacrifices of the Old Testament.

Part Two: The Impartation

I. Things to consider as you prepare:
  A. Aspects to bring out while teaching about the sacrifices.
    1. Reinforce the idea that from God's perspective, each time an animal sacrifice was made to atone for sin, God was looking forward to the day when the blood of His Son, Jesus, would make atonement once and for all, and the sacrificial system would come to an end.
        • Remind them that the blood of bulls and goats could never wash us from our sins. Their sacrifice looked forward to the day when Jesus, the Lamb of God, would be slain for our sin.
        • Remind them that Jesus died in our place; He took our punishment. Because of this, his blood washes us clean from our sin.

    2. As you describe each sacrifice, describe its purpose and a bit about how it was offered (adjust the "gory" content to the age and gender of your students—while girls don't usually enjoy "gore," you may find the boys pay more attention with a few "gory details.") Next, give its spiritual picture. They will remember better if you go sacrifice by sacrifice rather than waiting until the end and listing all the spiritual pictures.

  B. For this lesson, since it is more of a list, less of a story, we suggest that you use the model or large diagram of the tabernacle from the tabernacle lesson, and then make a large poster for each sacrifice, with the name of the sacrifice and a picture of what would be offered.

II. The Impartation: God commanded five types of sacrifices

A. The Burnt Offering

  1. Why it was offered (its purpose)

  2. What animals were offered

  3. What the person giving the offering did

  4. What the priest did

  5. The spiritual pictures in this offering

  6. Any other spiritual lessons to learn from this offering

B. The Grain Offering

1. Why it was offered (its purpose)

2. What was offered

3. How the person giving the offering prepared it

4. What the priest did

5. The spiritual pictures in this offering

6. Any other spiritual lessons to learn from this offering

C. The Fellowship Offering

1. Why it was offered (its purpose)

2. What animals were offered

3. What the person giving the offering did

4. What the priest did

5. The spiritual pictures in this offering

6. Any other spiritual lessons to learn from this offering

D. The Sin Offering

1. Why it was offered (its purpose)

2. What animals were offered

3. What the person giving the offering did

4. What the priest did

5. The spiritual pictures in this offering

6. Any other spiritual lessons to learn from this offering

E. The Trespass Offering

1. Why it was offered (its purpose)

2. What animals were offered

3. What the person giving the offering did

4. What the priest did

5. The spiritual pictures in this offering

6. Any other spiritual lessons to learn from this offering

Part Three: The Application

I. Explain that people had been sacrificing animals to God all along, starting with Adam and Eve and with Abel. That tradition had been passed down from generation to generation for hundreds of years. Pagan people sacrificed animals to their gods. Abraham sacrificed animals to the one true God, as did Isaac and Jacob. In Egypt, the children of Israel had watched the Egyptians sacrifice to their gods and goddesses. Now at this time, when God was forming the children of Israel into His chosen nation, God was explaining to the them, not only His laws for them, but the way they could be restored back to fellowship with Him if they broke those laws.

Discuss with your students how God set up the sacrificial system for two main reasons. First, it enabled the Israelites to restore their fellowship with God after they sinned. So for them it was an avenue to fellowship with God. Second, it was a picture for the people of Jesus' time and all of us after that to understand Jesus' death on our behalf. When John the Baptist saw Jesus and said to the men near him, "Look, there is the Lamb of God who is sent to take away the sins of the world," those men had a light pop on in their brains and in their spirits. They understood making a sacrifice for their own sins or for the sins of the nation. Now John was telling them that this man Jesus would die, not just for one person's sins or one nation's sins, but for everyone's sins, for the whole world.

Explain to your students that in many parts of the world, even today, people make animal sacrifices to false gods and to evil spirits. Those people don't think of their gods as false or of the spirits as evil. But the demons behind those false gods and evil spirits are robbing God of the worship that is due His name. In many countries and other religions, people do not know that Jesus offered His own life and His own blood as a better sacrifice than the sacrifice of bulls, goats, or lambs. One way to share the gospel with them is to explain that Jesus is the God-man who died once for all time so that they would not have to make those animal sacrifices, if they would only believe in Him.

II. Go on to share with your students some of what you learned about the sacrifice of Jesus from Hebrews 9 and 10:

   1.

   2.

   3.

   4.

   5.

III.   Writing in the student journals: if there is time, have students write their thoughts regarding these questions in their journals.

A. How do you think would have felt if your dad had to take a lamb from your farm to sacrifice for your sin? Why would you have felt like this?

B. How do you feel knowing that Jesus is the Lamb of God and He died for your sin? Why do you feel like this?

C. Did you understand this sacrifice picture of Jesus before this lesson? If not, does this help you understand Jesus' death better? What stuck out to you the most about this picture of the sacrifices?

Part Four: The Impact

A. Remind your students that God's purpose behind the sacrifices was not to kill animals. Remind them that God doesn't need to eat, nor does He gain strength from the offering or burning of the animals. Rather, God gave the sacrificial system as a prophetic picture so that we and Israel would understand the death of Jesus as sacrificially taking our punishment in our place. The sacrificial system also enforced the concept that redemption and forgiveness are costly; when we sin, someone gets hurt, someone must pay the price, someone must make restitution. When someone sins against us, and we forgive him, it is not without cost—we pay the cost by absorbing the injury committed. And if they can and do make restitution, then they have paid the price. The sacrifice system is a way of showing us that there is really never any "Get out of Jail Free" card—someone pays the price, whether it is the one who committed the sin, the one being sinned against, or an innocent person paying the price for the guilty person.

B. Talk about how great a price Jesus paid for us and why He was the only one who could pay it. Explain that God is infinite; that means we cannot measure Him. He has always been, and He always will be. There are no limits to Him. We are finite. We are limited in our time, in our strength; in every way, we are limited. Because we sinned and rebelled against an infinite God, the penalty is infinite and never-ending. Without Jesus, we would suffer punishment in the lake of fire for eternity. Jesus, who is fully God, became fully man. As the infinite God-man, He could take that infinite punishment on Himself for us, and because He himself is infinite, He could pay that infinite penalty in the instant moment of His death. He alone is the only one who could do this for us. No created being—no angel, no human—could do this. Only Jesus because He is the only God-man, fully God and fully man.

C. If there are any new students in your class, then you may want to give an invitation to accept Jesus' sacrifice and receive Him as Savior. If you have no new students, and you feel confident of the eternal state of each child's soul in your class, then wrap up the class with prayer.

Invite the children to join you in prayer.

Father, thank You for sending Your one and only Son, Jesus. Thank You, Jesus, that You humbled Yourself and became human, one of us, so that You could take our punishment upon Yourself. Thank You that You were obedient to Your Father every moment of every day so that You could be the sinless, perfect sacrifice for us. Thank You that by Your blood we can come boldly before the throne of God to ask for help when we need help. Thank You that by Your blood we are washed clean from our sin and guilt. Thank You, Father, that when You look at us, You see the righteousness of Jesus given to us. Thank You that in You, Jesus, we have been given everything that we need for life and godly living. Thank You that by Your wounds we are healed.

Pause here and ask if there are any children who want prayer for healing or for any other problems. Have them raise their hands. Invite children near them to lay hands on them and pray for them.

After a time of prayer, with you and your assistant teachers helping the students pray for one another, close in prayer.

D. End the class by encouraging your students to share with their family what they have learned today.

1. Encourage students to share with their families their thoughts about Jesus' sacrifice for us.
2. Encourage students to tell their families what they learned today about the O.T. sacrifices.
3. Encourage them to have their parents help them practice saying the five books of the Pentateuch and reciting the main events of Genesis, Exodus, and Leviticus with the hand motions.
4. Remind them about the at-home study pages at Forerunner Kids Club and encourage them to take a few minutes each day to work on them.

Questions to jump-start conversation with your 7- to 12-year-old on the way home from church:

1. What was the main topic of today's lesson? (Israel relates to God through the sacrifices)

2. What sacrifices do you remember?

3. What do the sacrifices teach us about Jesus?

Memory verse for this week:

"These are the regulations for the burnt offering, the grain offering, the sin offering, the guilt offering, the ordination offering, and the fellowship offering."
(Lev. 7:37)

Key thoughts to remember:
1. God set up the sacrificial system as a means for the people of God to atone for their sin, fellowship with Him, and give offerings to Him until Jesus made His sacrifice once for all.
2. God gave specific instructions for the sacrifices, because they are a picture about Jesus and His sacrifice for us.

THEME: *The Pentateuch*
Lesson 11: *Leviticus: Israel relates to God through the Sacrifices*

Day One: Leviticus 1

I. Read Leviticus 1. As you do, answer the following:

    1. What is the name of this first offering, in verse 3?

    2. What should he bring to offer?

    3. Where does a person go to present this offering to the Lord?

    4. When he gets there, what is the first thing he should do?

    5. What does he do next?

    6. What does the priest do with the blood?

    7. After the animal is cut into pieces, what is done with it?

    8. If the offering is a sheep or goat, what kind should it be?

    9. If the offering is a bird, what kind of bird should it be?

II.   Think about these things and write down your thoughts.

    1. Why do you think the person offering the sacrifice had to lay his hand on the head of the animal before sacrificing it?

    2. Verse 4 says that the sacrifice will make atonement for the one who offers it. Look up *atonement* and write the meaning down.

    3. How did Jesus make atonement for you?

At-Home Daily Activity Sheet 2

THEME: *The Pentateuch*
Lesson 11: *Leviticus: Israel relates to God through the Sacrifices*

Day Two: Leviticus 2

I. Read Leviticus 2. As you do, answer the following:

1. What is the name of this offering in verse 1?

2. What is this offering made of?

3. What is poured on it?

4. What is also offered with it?

5. What part is burned?

6. What is given to the priests?

7. If you want to bake your grain offering, of what do you make it?

8. What should *not* be in any grain offering?

9. In verse 13, with what should the offering be seasoned?

II.   Think about these things and write down your thoughts.

1. Read 1 Samuel 16:13. With what does Samuel anoint David? Who comes upon David with power? What do you think oil symbolizes?

2. Read Revelation 5:8. What does incense represent?

3. Read Luke 12:1. What does the yeast represent?

4. Read I Corinthians 5:8. What does the yeast represent?

5. What does I Corinthians 5:8 tell us about bread made without yeast? What does it represent?

THEME: *The Pentateuch*
Lesson 11: *Leviticus: Israel relates to God through the Sacrifices*

Day Three: Leviticus 3

I. Read Leviticus 3. As you do, answer the following:

1. What is the name of this offering?

2. What kind of herd animal may he offer?

3. Where does he offer it, and what must he do first?

4. What kind of lamb or goat may he offer?

5. Turn to Leviticus 7:11-36. In verses 12 and 16, what are the two reasons given for bringing a fellowship offering?

6. For a fellowship offering of thanksgiving, what else should be offered with it?

7. The fellowship offering is the only offering that the person offering it eats most of the meat. For a fellowship offering of thanksgiving, can some of the meat be kept to eat the next day? How about for the fellowship offering for a vow or made from one's freewill? Can leftovers be eaten the next day? Can it be eaten on the third day?

8. In verses 22-27, what parts of the animal may *not* be eaten?

9. In verses 31, what part of the animal do the priests get? _____ In verse 32, what part does the priest who burns the sacrifice get? _____

II.   Think about these things and write down your thoughts.

1. Think about why this offering is called a fellowship offering. Hint: God receives the burnt part. The priests receive some to eat. The officiating priest receives some to eat. The person who offers it receives most of it back to cook and eat with his family and friends. What kind of fellowship is going on?

2. This offering is not for redemption, but to show thankfulness to God, or when ending a vow, or just to show love to God. How important do you think this offering was to God? Why?

At-Home Daily Activity Sheet 4

THEME: *The Pentateuch*
Lesson 11: *Leviticus: Israel relates to God through the Sacrifices*

Day Four: Leviticus 4

I. Read Leviticus 4. As you do, answer the following:

1. When is this fourth offering made? For what does it atone?

2. What should a priest bring as a sin offering?

3. What should the whole community bring as a sin offering?

4. What should a leader bring as a sin offering?

5. What should a member of the community bring as a sin offering?

6. What is done with the blood of the sin offering?

II. Think about these things and write down your thoughts.

1. Did you notice that some people must bring an offering that costs more than others? Why do you think a leader has to bring a more costly offering than a "regular guy?" Why do you think a priest has to bring a more costly offering than a leader?

2. Do you think that the sins of those who bring more costly offerings are worse than the regular people's sins? Or do you think that because they are in positions of leadership, the consequences of their sins affect more people, so they need to bring a greater offering for atonement?

3. What does this say to us about being in leadership? If we are in leadership, how does our own personal sin affect those whom we lead?

THEME: *The Pentateuch*
Lesson 11: *Leviticus: Israel relates to God through the Sacrifices*

Day Five: Leviticus 5

I. Read Leviticus 5. As you do, answer the following:

1. This fifth offering is known as the trespass offering. What are the reasons given as to why it is offered?

    a. Verse 1:
    b. Verse 2:
    c. Verse 3:
    d. Verse 4:

2. In verse 6, what is brought as a trespass offering?

3. What if he can't afford a lamb? What should he bring?

4. What if he can't afford a pair of birds? What should he bring?

5. If he brings grain, does he put oil on it, representing the Holy Spirit?_____ Why do you think this is?

6. Verse 14 addresses the sin of accidentally misusing a holy item. What must he do to atone for this sin?

7. Verse 17 addresses the sin of breaking a command of God unintentionally (not on purpose, but by accident, or by not being aware of the command). What should be offered to atone for this sin?

II. Think about these things and write down your thoughts.

    1. Based on this offering, how important do you think it is to God that we defend someone we know is unfairly accused of a crime or that we testify to a crime that we know was committed?

    2. How serious was God about the Israelites not touching the things that God declared were unclean?

    3. How serious is God about people keeping a promise that they swear to keep?

First Quarter, Year One: Biblical Foundations for Children
Lesson Twelve:
Exodus: Israel Relates to God through the Feasts

Objective: to introduce the student to the Jewish feasts and the prophetic pictures in them.

Key verse for this lesson: "Speak to the Israelites and say to them: 'These are My appointed feasts, the feasts appointed by the Lord, which you are to proclaim as sacred assemblies.'" (Lev. 23:2)

Key thoughts to consider and to pass on:
1. God appointed the feasts so that He could celebrate with His people.
2. God designed the feasts to help Israel remember what He had done for them.
3. God also designed the feasts to be pictures of Jesus and His work of redemption.

Review from last week:

Outline of Leviticus

I.   Worship and sacrifices (ch. 1-16)
1.   Five kinds of sacrifices (ch. 1-7)
2.   The ordination and work of Israel's priests (ch. 8-10)
3.   Instructions for cleanliness and holiness (11-16)

II.   A holy lifestyle (ch. 17-27)
1.   Laws for all Israel (ch. 17-20)
2.   Laws for the priests (ch. 21-22)
3.   Seven festivals (ch. 23)
4.   Additional laws, penalties, and blessings (ch. 24-27

Biblical Foundation

I.   **Journaling through Leviticus 23**

A. Verse 2: what is God's other name for the appointed feasts?

B. What is the very first sacred assembly which God names? It's not a feast, but it happens every week.

C. The first feast is named in verse 5. What is it, when does it begin, and what does it commemorate?

D. What feast begins the very next day?

1. Why is it called that?

2. What do they do the first day?

3. What must they do each day?

4. What do they do the seventh day?

5. On which days may they work, and on which days may they not?

E. **The Feast of First Fruits** is described in verses 9-14.

1. What do the people bring to the priest on this day?

2. What does the priest do with this sheaf of grain?

Note: the first grain harvested each year was barley.

3. What other sacrifices do the people make that day?

4. Verse 14 mentions an offering which is new to us: the drink offering

a. What is the drink offering?

b. Genesis 35:14 is the first biblical reference to a drink offering. Who offers it and why?

c. Philippians 2:17: Paul refers to being poured out like a drink offering upon the sacrifices of other people. What is his mood here?

d. Look at Psalm 104:15 and Ecclesiastes 10:19. What do David and Solomon tell us is the purpose of wine?

e. In Deuteronomy 14:22-26, while Moses is rehearsing the laws and commands of the Lord for the people to remember when they come into the promised land, he addresses the harvest feast. He mentions that those living far away will have trouble bringing 10 percent of their harvest and animals to eat before the Lord at the tabernacle. In verse 25-26, he says to sell that 10 percent and bring the money (silver) to the tabernacle. Then he says, "Use the silver to buy whatever you like: cattle, sheep, wine or other fermented drink, or anything you wish. Then you and your family can eat there in the presence of God and rejoice with Him."

    f. Notice that wine brings joy and is used in rejoicing. The levitical directions for the sacrifices for the atonement did not contain a drink offering. It is after we have been reconciled with God that we can rejoice with Him in the completion of the work and in the restoration of relationship. So the drink offering represents joy in the completed work of God.

5. Notice the command given in verse 14. When they begin to harvest the first grain that ripened, they were to bring the very first sheaf, *and* they were *not* to eat any of this new grain, whether made into bread, or roasted, or even eaten raw, *until* the first sheaf had been offered before the Lord and they celebrated with Him the harvest to come. Notice this is not the giving of the tithe. This is only one sheaf, and it is brought to God first to acknowledge that all provision comes from Him.

F. **The Feast of Weeks:** The next feast is held seven weeks after First Fruits, hence the name "the Feast of Weeks." Because one counted off seven weeks from the very day of the feast of firstfruits, one was counting that "day after the Sabbath" twice—once at the beginning and once at the end. Hence, fifty days, but seven weeks.

    1. What are they to bring? Go ahead and list it all:

    2. Why? Because there are a lot of sacrifices to make:
       a. A burnt offering together with grain offerings and drink offerings
       b. A sin offering
       c. A fellowship offering
       d. Lastly, the offering of the bread made from the harvest grain

    3. Who gets the wave offering of the lamb breast, right thigh, and the bread?

    4. The family feasts on the remainder of the lamb fellowship offering, plus any other bread they've brought, vegetables or fruit from the garden or local market, and then wine to celebrate.

       a. Deuteronomy 14:22-23 tells us that they bring a tithe of their harvest: grain, new wine, oil, and the firstborn of the flocks and herds.

b. Deuteuronomy 16:10-11 tells us that they brought freewill offerings in proportion to the harvest with which God had blessed them. It also tells us that the Feast of Weeks was a time for great rejoicing for everyone, even the servants and the foreigners.

G. The Feast of Trumpets

1. Verse 23: when does this feast take place?
2. How long is it?
3. What do they do?

H. The Day of Atonement

1. Verse 27: when does this feast take place?

2. "Deny yourselves" means to fast. So is this a day of feasting or fasting?

3. Is there an offering made?

4. How serious was God about people *not* working on this day?

5. Turn back to Leviticus 16 and read it. This describes the events of the day in great detail, especially concerning the duties of the high priest and the sacrifices made that day.

   a. What must the high priest wear?

   b. What does he offer first? For whom does it make atonement?

In other words, the priest must first receive atonement before he can represent the people before the Lord.

   c. What animal is offered next?

   d. Why are there two of these presented? What happens concerning them?

   e. The one not chosen to become the sacrifice becomes the goat who escapes or the "scapegoat." What is done concerning him? That is, what do they do with him before leading him into the wilderness?

   f. How often was this sacrifice to atone for all the sins of all the Israelites offered?

I. The Feast of tabernacles

1. Verse 34: when does this feast take place?

2. How many days?

3. Where do the people live?

4. Are there offerings made?

5. How are the first and eighth days similar?

6. Verse 43: What does this feast commemorate?

II. Symbolism in the Feasts

A. Passover:
1. As we discussed in Exodus, the Passover lamb symbolizes Jesus, who died in our place.
2. The blood marked on the top of the door frame and on either side represents the cross on which He died.

B. Feast of Unleavened Bread:
1. Symbolizes Jesus, who said, "I am the bread of life" (Jn. 6:48).
2. No leaven is to be used in the bread nor should any be in the house at all. Leaven symbolizes sin and false teaching. Unleavened bread symbolizes living a righteous life before the Lord.
3. Another picture of Jesus regarding bread: He was born in Bethlehem, which means "house of bread."
4. Unleavened bread not only is made without yeast, but it is rolled flat and pricked all over so that the steam escapes and the bread does not rise. The finished product has stripes of burned places where the bread cooked on the stones or oven. These stripes remind us of Jesus, who was beaten before being crucified; by His stripes we are healed. The holes pricked and pierced into the bread reminds us of His head, which was pricked by the crown of thorns and that He was pierced for our transgressions.

C. The Feast of Firstfruits:
1. Jesus was raised from the dead on the Feast of Firstfruits.
2. Jesus is referred to as the first fruit, the firstborn from the dead (1 Cor. 15:20-23).
3. In John 12:23-24, Jesus likens his death to being the seed which must be sown into the ground and die before it produces fruit. This makes Jesus the firstfruit, given to

the Lord and sown in death to produce new life in us.

D. The Feast of Weeks:

1. This is the feast that we know as Pentecost, from the Greek word meaning "fiftieth," because it was celebrated on the fiftieth day after the Feast of Firstfruits.

2. It was on Pentecost, the day when the Feast of Weeks was being held, that the Holy Spirit first came upon the apostles and other believers in the upper room where they had been praying for ten days.

3. At the Feast of Weeks, the Israelites were celebrating the completion of the harvest. On Pentecost, in Acts 2, we see the completion of the redemptive work of Christ as the Holy Spirit is first given to the believers as the down payment—as the engagement ring, as it were—for our marriage to Jesus, our Bridegroom.

E. The Feast of Trumpets:

1. On this day, the priest sounds the trumpet, and everyone everywhere stops what they are doing to come to the solemn assembly. Even those laboring in the field would stop their labor immediately to come to the tabernacle or temple.

2. In the Old Testament, the sounding of the trumpet called people to battle or to worship. The sounding of the trumpet was a call to awareness and readiness.

    a. The trumpet sound calls us to battle. This reminds us of the spiritual warfare which Paul described in Ephesians 6.

    b. We know that Jesus commands the army of heaven.

3. In the New Testament, the sounding of the trumpet refers to the judgments of God in the book of Revelation and the return of Christ at the last trumpet.

4. The first four feasts have had fulfillment in Christ. The feast of trumpets awaits fulfillment in Christ; it will be fulfilled when Jesus returns at the sound of the trumpet of God.

5. This feast became known as Rosh Hashanah: the head of the year. Even though it is not celebrated in the first month of the Jewish year, but in the seventh month, it has come to be Jewish New Year's Day because it begins ten days of reflection and repentance that leads into the Day of Atonement.

F. The Day of Atonement:

1. Although included in the feasts, it is a day of fasting, a day of solemn assembly.

2. Although the high priest had to make atonement first for his own sins, Hebrews 7:27 reminds us that Jesus did not have to make atonement for Himself before making atonement for us; He was perfect, without sin.

3. Both goats are a picture of Jesus.

    a. The goat that was slain is a picture of the death of Jesus, the blood sacrifice that made atonement for us.

    b. The goat over whom the sins were recited and who then carried the sins far away, represents Jesus, who took our sins upon Himself and carried them far from us.

4. Notice that this sacrifice is a goat, not a lamb. The goat symbolizes the sinner, and Jesus was made sin for us; He was identified as a sinner so that we could be identified as having been made holy.

5. This day is a day of judgment. In the sense of judgment, it too, awaits fulfillment in Christ. When the earth experiences the great and terrible day of the Lord, it will be a day of judgment for the unsaved, but a day of salvation for the redeemed of the Lord.

G. The Feast of tabernacles:

1. This feast takes place just five days after the Day of Atonement. It is perhaps the most joyful of the feasts. So after a day of fasting and repentance, just five days later God shows His mercy and His joy in the restored relationship with His people by having them celebrate with a week-long campout!

2. It happens after the harvest is completed. This may well await fulfillment in Christ as it may symbolize the thousand-year reign of Christ on earth, which takes place after the end-time harvest.

III. Finish these sentences:

1. The feast that impacted me the most was _____ because . . .

2. What interested me the most about the annual feasts was . . .

3. What bothered me the most about the annual feasts was . . .

4. I would most like to attend the feast of _____ because . . .

5. I like thinking about Jesus as my scapegoat because . . .

6. If I were an Israelite farmer, and I had to go to Jerusalem to wave the first sheaf of my harvest, I would feel . . .

7. The most interesting "feast fact" to me was . . .

THEME: *The Pentateuch*
Lesson 12: *Leviticus: Israel relates to God through the Feasts*

Part One: The Invitation

A. Review:

    1. Unit theme: God is a Father who desires a family.

    2. Lead your students in reciting the names of the five books of the Pentateuch.

    3. Lead your students in reciting the main events of Genesis, Exodus, and Leviticus, with hand motions:

Creation	Abraham	Moses	Red Sea
Fall	Isaac	"Let my people go!"	Mt. Sinai
Flood	Jacob	"No!"	10 Commandments
Tower of Babel	Joseph	Ten Plagues	tabernacle
Nations scatter	To Egypt	Passover	

Priests
Five sacrifices
Seven festivals
Holy living

B. Introduce today's lesson topic and explain that God gave the Israelites instructions about solemn assemblies or feasts when they were to come together before Him.

C. Share the key verse for this lesson with your students: "Speak to the Israelites and say to them: 'These are My appointed feasts, the feasts appointed by the Lord, which you are to proclaim as sacred assemblies'" (Lev. 23:2).

Explain that there were seven feasts, that each had their own purpose, and that today we are going to learn about these feasts and how we can see Jesus through the pictures that they make. Mention that:

    1. God appointed the feasts so that He could celebrate with His people.
    2. God designed the feasts to help Israel remember what He had done for them.
    3. God also designed the feasts to be pictures of Jesus and His work of redemption.

D. Invite your students to meet with God and His desire for relationship with them through the feasts of the Old Testament.

Part Two: The Impartation

I. Things to consider as you prepare:
    A. Aspects to bring out while teaching about the feasts.
        1. These were called "solemn assemblies" by the Lord. That means they were a time for the Israelite people to come together for a special and often serious purpose.
        2. While the sacrifices dealt with restoring one's relationship with God so that one could fellowship with God, the feasts dealt mainly with remembering what God had done or celebrating what He was doing.
        3. As you describe each feast, describe its purpose and how it was celebrated. Next, give its spiritual picture. They will remember better if you go feast by feast rather than waiting until the end and listing all the spiritual pictures.
    B. For this lesson, since it is more of a list and less of a story, we suggest that you make a large poster for each feast, with the name of the feast and a picture that represents it.

II. The Impartation: God commanded seven annual feast or solemn assemblies

A. Passover

1. Quick reminder of the Passover:
    ii. Lamb slain and roasted; blood put on doorposts and lintel
    iii. Unleavened bread
    iv. Bitter herbs to remember their suffering

2. The picture of Jesus in the Passover:

3. How we relate to this feast today:

B. Feast of Unleavened Bread

1. When it was and how long it lasted:

2. What they did:

3. The spiritual pictures in this feast:

C. The Feast of First Fruits:

1. When it was:

2. What they did:

3. The spiritual pictures in this feast:

D. The Feast of Weeks:

1. When it was:

2. What they did:

3. The spiritual pictures in this feast:

E. The Feast of Trumpets

1. When it was:

2. What they did:

3. The spiritual pictures in this feast:

F. The Day of Atonement

1. When it was:

2. What they did:

3. The spiritual pictures in this feast:

G. The Feast of tabernacles

1. When it was and how long it lasted:

2. What they did (maybe you might bring in a pre-fabricated booth that they could put together and then put branches on top):

3. The spiritual pictures in this feast:

Part Three: The Application

I. Pick an activity:
  A. Drawing: provide your students with paper and crayons. Have them draw themselves celebrating one of the feasts. Encourage them to pick the feast they think they would like the most or the feast through which God spoke the most to them.
  B. Acting: break the class out into smaller groups and assign each one a feast to act out. Give them five minutes to prepare, then let each group act out their feast.
  C. Feast charades: ask for volunteers to come up to act out a feast and have the other students guess which feast it is.

II. Writing in the student journals: If there is time, have students write their thoughts regarding these questions in their journals.

  A. What is your favorite picture of Jesus in the feasts?

  B. What do you think it would be like to grow up in a small nation where everyone got together at least three times a year for a feast? Do you think you would enjoy it? Why?

  C. Do you think that God likes to use pictures to tell us about Himself and about what will happen. For example, Jesus rose from the dead on the feast of first fruits and the Holy Spirit fell upon the apostles and the brand-new church on the feast of weeks. What does it tell you about God that He likes to speak to us in pictures and symbols?

Part Four: The Impact

  A. Remind your students that God gave the Israelites these feasts so that they could come together as His family to celebrate with Him and remember all that He had done and was doing for them. The purpose of the feasts was fellowship with God and with each other. We believers also have a special feast which Jesus gave us from the Passover. The last time He was celebrating the Passover with His disciples, He took the unleavened bread and He told them, "This is My body, which is broken for you." Then He took the Passover wine cup, and He told them, "This is My blood, which is shed for you." And then He told them that whenever they ate the bread and drank the cup, they would be remembering His death until He came again. We call this "the Lord's Supper" because Jesus was eating the Passover supper when He gave these instructions. We also call it "communion." "Communion" means "to fellowship with." So when we eat the bread that reminds us of how the body of Jesus was broken for us and we drink the cup which reminds us of His blood that was shed for us, we are communing with Jesus—we are fellowshipping with Him. We are also feasting in such a way that we remember what He did and what He still is doing for us.

  Note: when you teach this, hold up the elements of the communion table. You might want to use real unleavened bread. You might also use a wine glass with juice in it to represent the cup, so that it looks more like what Jesus used, instead of those little plastic communion cups.

Invite the children to join you in remembering Jesus' death and resurrection as you take communion together. Be sure to have prepared a plate of broken unleavened bread and small paper or plastic cups of juice. Lead first in the prayer over the bread, thanking Jesus for His body broken for us. Next lead in prayer for the cup, the shed blood of Jesus. Close by thanking Jesus that through His death we are forgiven. Thank Him that we can fellowship with Him and with His Father.

If there is time, you might pause here and ask if there are any children who want prayer for healing or for any other problems. Have them raise their hands. Invite children near them to lay hands on them and pray for them.

After a time of prayer, with you and your assistant teachers helping the students pray for one another, close in prayer.

B. End the class by encouraging your students to share with their family what they have learned today.

    1. Encourage students to tell their families what they learned today about the O.T. feasts.

    2. Encourage them to have their parents help them practice saying the five books of the Pentateuch and reciting the main events of Genesis, Exodus, and Leviticus with the hand motions.

    3. Remind them about the at-home study pages at Forerunner Kids Club and encourage them to take a few minutes each day to work on them.

Questions to jump-start conversation with your 7- to 12-year-old on the way home from church:

1. What was the main topic of today's lesson? (Israel relates to God through the feasts)

2. What feast do you remember?

3. Which feast do you wish you could celebrate? Why is that?

Memory verse for this week:
> "Speak to the Israelites and say to them: 'These are My appointed feasts, the feasts appointed by the Lord, which you are to proclaim as sacred assemblies.'" (Lev. 23:2)

Key thoughts to consider and to pass on:
1. God appointed the feasts so that He could celebrate with His people.
2. God designed the feasts to help Israel remember what He had done for them.
3. God also designed the feasts to be pictures of Jesus and His work of redemption.

At-Home Daily Activity Sheet 1

THEME: *The Pentateuch*
Lesson 11: *Leviticus: Israel relates to God through the Sacrifices*

Day One: Leviticus 23:1-8

I. Read Leviticus 23:1-8. As you do, answer the following:

1. In verse 3, we read about a special day that is not a feast, but it is a day of sacred assembly. What did the Lord call it?

2. What is the first feast mentioned in verse 5?

3. When does this feast take place?

4. What is the name of the second feast?

5. When does this feast begin?

6. How many days does it last?

7. What do they do on the first day?

8. What do they do every day?

9. What do they do the last day of the feast?

10. Read Exodus 12:15-20. Why is this called the Feast of Unleavened bread? What must not be in their houses for seven days?

II.   Think about these things and write down your thoughts.

1.   What did the Feast of Unleavened Bread help the Israelites remember?

2.   From last week's lessons, what do you remember yeast might represent?

3.   Why do you think God had them get rid of all the yeast once a year? What do you think He was reminding them?

THEME: *The Pentateuch*
Lesson 11: *Leviticus: Israel relates to God through the Sacrifices*

Day Two: Leviticus 23:9-14

I. Read Leviticus 23:9-14. As you do, answer the following:

1. Was this feast celebrated during the forty years in the desert? How do you know?

2. This feast is related to the harvest time. At what time of the harvest is this celebrated?

3. What do they bring to the priest?

4. What does he do with it?

5. What day do they do this?

6. What offerings do they make with this "wave offering?"
   a. A burnt offering of _____
   b. A grain offering of _____
   c. A drink offering of _____

7. What may they not do with the new grain until they do all this?

8. Once they get to the promised land, they begin celebrating this annually. Is this for their generation only?

II. Think about these things and write down your thoughts.

1. Notice that verse 10 says it is a sheaf of the first grain that they harvest. Once the Israelites reached the promised land, they harvested several grains each year. The first grain to ripen was the barley. After the barley harvest came the wheat harvest. Why do you think God wanted them to wave a sheaf of grain from the first harvest in His presence *before* they could eat from the new harvest? What did this teach or remind them?

2. For those who lived far from the tabernacle (and later the temple), they were not required to come to the tabernacle to do this. Look at Deuteronomy 16:16. All the men had to travel to the tabernacle (or temple) for just three times, for four of these feasts: Passover/Feast of Unleavened Bread, the Feast of Weeks (at the end of the harvest), and the Feast of Tabernacles. So the Feast of Firstfruits was performed by the priest, on behalf of the people. Read 1 Corinthians 15:20-23. Who is our Firstfruit?

THEME: *The Pentateuch*
Lesson 11: *Leviticus: Israel relates to God through the Sacrifices*

Day Three: Leviticus 23:15-22

I. Read Leviticus 23:15-22. As you do, answer the following:

1. How did the Israelites find the start date of the fourth feast? (We call this Pentecost; the Israelites called it the Feast of Weeks).

2. In the wave offering, a sheaf of new grain was waved before the Lord. According to verse 17, how is the new grain waved before the Lord at this feast?

3. So each family brings two loaves of bread, made with yeast, to wave before the Lord. In verse 18, what else does the priest offer on behalf of the nation?

4. In verses 19-20, what does the priest offer on his own behalf?

5. According to verse 21, what kind of day is this? Is it a normal kind of day?

6. Look at verse 22. In the middle of talking about the special celebrations, God gives them a command. This is a feast about the harvest, and this command is also about the harvest. What is the command?

7. What does this verse show us about God's concern for the poor?

8. Is God telling them to give food to the poor, or to leave grain unharvested in the field for the poor people to harvest?

II.   Think about these things and write down your thoughts.

1. Notice that this grain offering contains yeast, which often represents sin, and then the feast also includes animal sacrifices to atone for sin. Why do you think God is reminding them about sin and forgiveness in this festival that celebrates His providing for them through the harvest? (Hint: Look at Genesis 3:17-18.)

2. How great is God's heart to provide for the poor that He interrupts the discussions of the feasts to give instructions for their provision! Perhaps He is reminding the people, "I provide for you in the harvest; you use some of your harvest, which you worked hard for, to provide the opportunity for those who have no land to work for their own harvest." What do you think? And, what do you think about God requiring the poor to do some labor for this provision? They have to harvest this grain left for them.

THEME: *The Pentateuch*
Lesson 11: *Leviticus: Israel relates to God through the Sacrifices*

Day Four: Leviticus 23:23-32

I. Read Leviticus 23:23-32. As you do, answer the following:

1. When does this fifth feast take place?

2. What do they do this day?

3. Are there any offerings? Does God specify what to offer, or is this a day when they offer what they want (that is, a freewill offering)?

4. Since it is a freewill offering, that means it is a fellowship offering. So what does that tell you they spent the day doing?

5. What is the name of the next feast or special day? When is it?

6. What do they do on this day?

7. Read Leviticus 16 and write down what the high priest had to do on the day of atonement to make atonement for himself and for the people:

    a. What did he sacrifice for himself?
    b. What did he sacrifice for the people?
    c. To what special place he take the blood from this sacrifice?
    d. What happened to the "scapegoat" (Lev. 16:21-22)?

II.   Think about these things and write down your thoughts.

1. The feast when they blow trumpets is called "the feast of trumpets." Look up these verses to see what sounding the trumpet represents.

    Nehemiah 4:20
    Isaiah 27:13
    Jeremiah 4:5

2. Read Hebrews 9:11-14. How was the Day of Atonement a picture of what Christ would do for us?

At-Home Daily Activity Sheet 5

THEME: *The Pentateuch*
Lesson 11: *Leviticus: Israel relates to God through the Sacrifices*

Day Five: Leviticus 23:33-44

I. Read Leviticus 23:33-44. As you do, answer the following:

1. What is the name of the seventh feast?

2. When is it? How long does it last?

3. Do they present offerings during this feast?

4. Since God doesn't tell them what to offer, they are offering fellowship freewill offerings, aren't they? This means that they can keep the leftover meat to eat on the second day. So a family (or group of families) would sacrifice on one day, eat the meat of that fellowship offering for two days, then make another offering to eat for another two days, and so on.

5. According to verse 40, what do they do during this feast?

6. Look at verses 42-43. Where do they live during this feast?

7. What does God want them to remember during this feast?

8. According to verse 39, have they finished harvesting all their crops by this time? _____ So is this like a week-long vacation at the end of working hard to plant, cultivate, and harvest?

II.   Think about these things and write down your thoughts.

1. Of all seven feasts, which one seems to be the most fun?

2. What does it tell you about God that He planned for His people to take a week every year as a fun camping vacation, with lots of food and people?

3. The Day of Atonement was the most holy and serious day of the year for the Israelites. They had to fast all day, and they mourned over their sin. Just five days later, God plans for them to take this week-long, fun vacation. What does that tell you about how God feels about us when we confess our sin? Read 1 John 1:7-9.

Instructions for preparation of the Timeline.

Photocopy the timeline pages. We recommend that you laminate them. Attach the timeline segments to one another in chronological order as you fasten them to the wall of your classroom. Lessons that use timeline pictures instruct you which pictures to hang at which points on the timeline.

Here's a source for timeline pictures if you have Microsoft Word:

http://office.microsoft.com/en-us/clipart/results.aspx?qu=Bible&sc=20

If you go to this URL, then all the Microsoft Word Bible pictures come up, and you can download the ones you want for:

Adam and Eve
Cain and Abel
Noah
Abraham
Moses

Install them in MS Word so that you can insert them as pictures into a blank document. You may have to resize them before printing. (If you line them up two pictures wide by three pictures down, they will print out at a nice size.) You can then cut out and laminate the pictures.

BEFORE
4000 B.C.

3000 B.C.

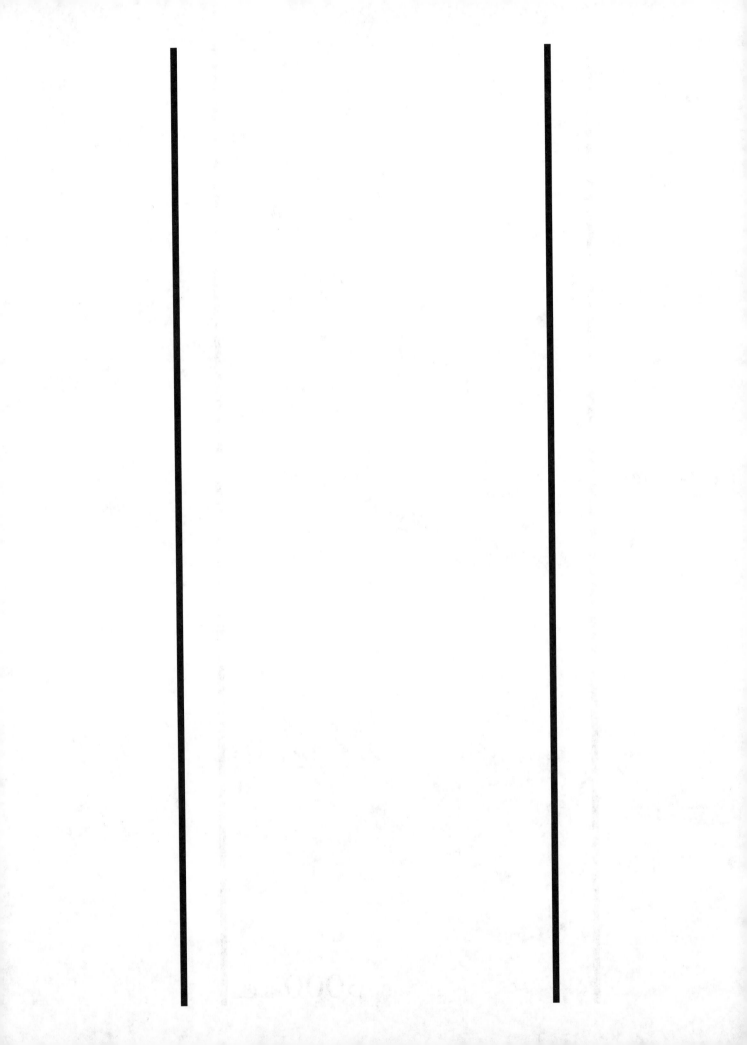

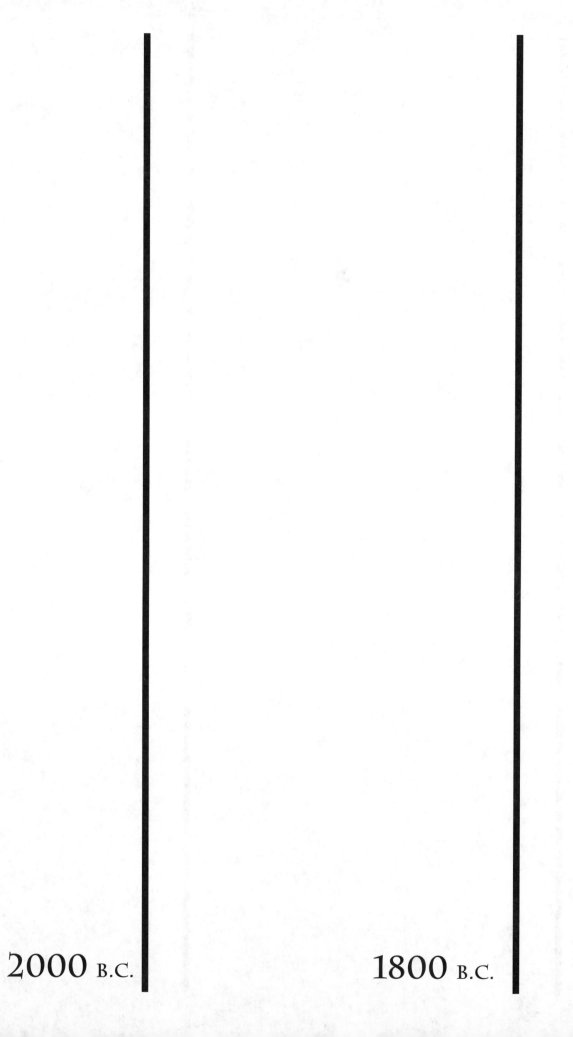

2000 B.C.   1800 B.C.

1600 B.C. |

1400 B.C. |

1200 B.C.   1000 B.C.

800 B.C.

600 B.C.

400 B.C.   200 B.C.

0 B.C.   A.D. 200

A.D. 400

A.D. 600

A.D. 800 | A.D. 1000 |

A.D. 1200 | A.D. 1400 |

A.D. 1600 |

A.D. 1800 |

A.D. 2000

MIKEBICKLE.org

FREE Resource Library

This library comprises a wealth of resources from over 25 years of Mike's teaching ministry and provides access to hundreds of resources in various formats, including streaming video, downloadable video, and audio, accompanied by study notes and transcriptions—absolutely free of charge. Here you will find some of Mike's most beloved titles, including *The Life of David, The Song of Songs, The First Commandment, The Book of Romans, The Book of Revelation,* and much more. Mike has always encouraged people to freely copy and share his teachings, so we encourage you to take full advantage of these resources and share them widely with your friends and family: *"Our copyright is the right to copy."* New content is continually being prepared and expanded from Mike's archives, and all new teachings will be added immediately.

Subscribe to Mike Bickle's FREE video podcast.

internships

Encounter God. Do His Works. Change the World.

Each of our four internships are committed to praying for the release of the fullness of God's power and purpose as interns actively win the lost, heal the sick, feed the poor, and minister in the power of the Holy Spirit. Our vision is to work in relationship with the larger Body of Christ to serve the Great Commission, as we seek to walk out the two great commandments to love God and people. Our desire is to see each intern build strong relationships and lifelong friendships.

INTRO TO IHOP–KC

A 3-month program for those joining IHOP–KC staff. This program offers classes about IHOP–KC's values, ministries, and structure, and gives practical skills for you to succeed long-term as an intercessory missionary. This program is designed for both families and singles.

ONE THING

A 6-month program for single young adults.

SIMEON COMPANY

A 3-month program for those 50 years and over, whether married or single.

FIRE IN THE NIGHT

A 3-month program for young adults between the ages of 18–30 who cry out to the Lord between the hours of midnight and 6:00am.

International House of Prayer University
3535 E. Red Bridge Road, Kansas City, MO 64137
816.763.0200 • internships@ihop.org • IHOP.org/internships

INTERNATIONAL HOUSE OF PRAYER
MISSIONS BASE OF KANSAS CITY

Combining 24/7 Prayers for Justice
with 24/7 Works of Justice

Since September 19, 1999, we have continued in night and day prayer with worship as the foundation of our ministry to win the lost, heal the sick, and make disciples as we labor alongside the larger Body of Christ to serve the Great Commission and to live as forerunners who prepare the way for the return of Jesus. By the grace of God, we are committed to combining 24/7 prayers for justice with 24/7 works for justice until the Lord returns. We are best equipped to reach out to others when our lives are rooted in prayer that focuses on intimacy with God and intercession for a breakthrough of the fullness of God's power and purpose for this generation.

For more information on our internships, conferences, university, live prayer room webcast, and more, please visit our website at IHOP.org.

International House of Prayer Missions Base
3535 E. Red Bridge Road, Kansas City, MO 64137
816.763.0200 • info@ihop.org • IHOP.org

INTERNATIONAL HOUSE OF PRAYER UNIVERSITY

Encounter God. Do His Works. Change the World.

Forerunner School of Ministry
Forerunner Music Academy
Forerunner Media Institute
eSchool & Distance Learning

IHOPU's mandate is to equip and send out believers who love Jesus and others wholeheartedly, to preach the Word, heal the sick, serve the poor, plant churches and start houses of prayer, and proclaim the return of Jesus.

IHOPU stands in an environment of 24/7 prayer with worship and a thriving missions base. We are establishing a community built around the centrality of Scripture, prayer, and worship in a context where the Word of God is continuously expressed through teaching, singing, praying, and ministry to one another.

International House of Prayer University
3535 E. Red Bridge Road, Kansas City, MO 64137
816.763.0243 • ihopu@ihop.org • IHOP.org/university